Let's Talk Polo Ponies…

Sunny Hale

DEDICATION

I dedicate this book to all of the horses that have played such an important role in my life and polo career. Without you, I would never have known just how far one person could go in this world. I will always be in gratitude for the gift you brought and the journey we have shared in pursuit of achieving my dream in the sport of Polo.

Copyright Sunny Hale 2016

All rights reserved. No part of this work may be reproduced in any form without the written consent of its author.

www.sunnyhalepolo.com

1
A Personal Note From Sunny…*1*

2
Your Greatest Team Mate…*9*

3
Step One to Steady Progress…*19*

4
Are You Matched Up Correctly?…*53*

5
How Strong is Your String? …*75*

6
Tips on Buying Polo Ponies…*89*

7
Tips on Buying Prospects…*125*

8
Tips on Playing Unknown Horses …*147*

9
Now Let's Talk About You…*159*

10
Who is Sunny Hale…*167*

Let's Talk Polo book series available at:
amazon.com/author/Sunnyhale

For more Polo tips follow:
Instagram / Lets Talk Polo
Facebook /Lets Talk Polo

Now let's get to it…

WARNING

Polo is addicting…fact.

Polo horses are even more addicting…fact.

If you buy one polo horse…you will need a second one.

This will be the greatest addiction you will ever have.

www.sunnyhalepolo.com

1

A personal note from Sunny…

Welcome to the book I couldn't wait to write! Polo ponies are one of my absolute favorite things about Polo and a HUGE subject to cover. For that reason I decided to address the topic one angle at a time so that I could really give the reader the full benefits of knowing as much a possible. I also want to be able to truly give polo ponies the credit they deserve when it comes to the success of a polo player and that takes time to explain properly. As an aspiring polo player there are certain things you need to understand clearly that will be the foundation of your future success. This is one of absolute first and key elements to know when it comes to polo ponies.

> The horses you play will be the foundation of your success or failure as a polo player.

Trust me on that statement…it is a fact. It is also crucial that you understand clearly and be able to determine which horses specifically will bring you the most success and will add to your rate of growth in the sport and which ones are holding you back. This is the point of this first book. It is about you and the horses you are working with and will choose to work with. This is information you cannot be without if you mean to reach your best potential as a player. This first book is really more about you the player and the discovery of the hidden information that is at the root of all great players and their horses. So get ready, there is no book like it that has this kind of insider information. Think of this information to come like seeing the wizard behind the curtain at a magic show. This is the magic behind all great players that leaves you in awe as you watch them perform on the field. This book will help you see the horse connection top players are aware of that the average player is not.

Getting to the top in Polo takes a lot of dedication and hard work implementing solid strategies. The first step is knowing you are dealing with the right information and the second step is implementing that information in your daily work ethic. That is the best formula I know for success and that is exactly what I would like to hand you by the end of this book. I would like to hand you the information about polo ponies that you can apply to your own situation that will help improve on what you already know and give you the opportunity to expand your growth in the areas you may have been struggling with due to the lack of the right information. To know you are dealing with the right information, you have to be able to use the info repeatedly and get the same or better results. That is what reaching for the top of anything is all about. That is the professional wisdom I will explain for you in the pages ahead, so get ready these are tried and tested methods that I used to reach the top and conquer my dream in the sport, so I know they work. This is highly specialized information that is simple to understand when you know what to look for. This is the information about polo ponies that can help you reach your best potential. These concepts are also shared by the top players in the world and can be witnessed by entering any one of their barn aisles and taking a look at what is there in their horses. There is a definite common ground in why the top players are able to achieve that kind of success and that is what I am going to explain to you in this first book on polo ponies. How you too can get there in your own horse organization, no matter how small or large it may be, if you are willing to do the work in applying the information one small step at a time.

I hope you enjoy the information and find it to be extremely useful. Is this the only book I will write on the subject of polo ponies? Absolutely not, I will confess. I have a serious addiction to horses that will take years to explain on paper fully so keep an eye out for new releases as the book series unfolds ☺! In fact that is what the Let's Talk Polo book series is all about. A library of books on Polo and the wisdom behind succeeding in the sport, so just consider this book #1 on the subject of polo ponies. Additionally you should know, that the reason I felt it should be the priority in the release is because of how important the benefits could be to the reader who does not have access to top professionals for this kind of advice. Your wisdom and understanding of your horses is everything to your advancement in the sport. After you have this kind of wisdom, it is about daily implementation in your work ethic with your horses to reach success. Polo ponies can make or break you as a player and that is what I want to help explain, so you can do your best and truly enjoy the experience to the fullest as I have.

If you will start paying attention to the finer details and concepts that I will explain for you in this book, you will begin to see the potential for steady progress in areas that used to be untouchable. The details I will explain take time to work into your program, but I assure you of one thing. The overall benefits you will start to receive will show in areas you couldn't seem to make progress in before and may have been the actual culprit behind holding you back from steady improvement in the sport. Well not any longer. My goal at the end of this book is for you to understand clearly how much there is to gain in the relationship you have with your horses when you get it right and some straight forward advice that will help you in the purchasing department so you can skip some of those expensive mistakes that are all too common. Some of these details there are zero resources for so good on you for buying this book…your opponent may not have found it yet! ☺

Always remember, the connection you have and will have with the world's greatest athlete…the polo pony…is a powerful journey of transformation for both of you. Enjoy the journey.

Now let's get started ☺!

Sunny

2

Your Greatest Team Mate

Photo: High Roller (aka: Tricky Lil Dude) AQHA/TB gelding raised, trained and played by Sunny.

Let's start from the beginning and the absolute foundation of all to come regarding your future success in the sport of Polo. Everything you can accomplish on the polo field as a player comes down to what the horse is willing to do for you…or not. That may sound funny, but it is the absolute truth. Within your personal team there is one teammate who you will need to completely understand, respect and become one with in order to reach the absolute top of your game. Not sure what I mean exactly? Let me simplify it for you. Who helps you get to the end line to save a ball that is going out? Who lets you pass the player in the front of the pack with the ball so you can make a back shot to your teammates in defense? Who helps you have confidence when you are taking the 30-yard open goal penalty shot to win the game in overtime? Who helps you be able to take out the opponent you have been assigned to that is higher ranked than you? Who allows you to pass the entire pack on a run to goal to win a game? Who allows you to push and hold a line against a much bigger horse that means a 30-yard open goal penalty that can win the tied game? Who gives you the power and freedom to explore your curiosities and take steps of advancement in the sport to higher and faster levels? That teammate is your polo pony.

You can have an average relationship with your human teammates and still sneak by if you're lucky, but your polo pony is who will give you wings or leave you planted on the ground...literally. The polo pony is your greatest asset on the field and the one responsible for your greatest enjoyment of the game. That is the teammate you should get to know, because that is the one who will carry you to your highest potential as a polo player. If the horse is on your side and in the game with you, there is no other feeling or power like it. You are talking about access to magic on hooves if you will take the time to appreciate them and where they are coming from. Giving time to getting to know them and what makes them tick is a strategy you need to work on as a polo player and that means each day in your actual follow through about seeking knowledge that will improve the relationship and the advancement of your personal riding and horsemanship skills. If you are not willing to take a deeper look into your greatest teammate and the relationship you have with them, by your daily actions, then I assure you of one thing. You will ALWAYS be limited in your potential to improve, no way around it. Sure, you can get away with a weak chukker here or there and fib through a few plays helping a tough horse get around, but an overall disrespect for the world's greatest athlete in your attitude, that it just doesn't really matter that much, will kill your potential as a polo player who had visions of being great. That attitude will help you lose lots of games and adds up to a whole lot of frustration on the polo field when you can't quite get to that ball you were chasing or you can't quite get your horse to slow down for that slow rolling ball coming at you from behind. From all angles it matters. Horses can help you or you can try to do it alone.

Did you know that a horse has a choice to run the goal post over or step to the side as you reach out to make that oh so important goal? The ones, who trust you and are in the battle with you, will step right through it for you. Wouldn't you like to know how to reach that level of help, instead of some nice green road rash on your whites? That is where your relationship, pursuit of knowledge and daily execution of the right knowledge counts. How much you are able to get out of the relationship is up to you and depends on how much you are willing to put into it. Wouldn't you like the horse to be thinking for you and attempting to help the situation? I know I would.

Always remember this one piece of advice. The horse is everything to your success on the field and they have a lot to share with you if you will just slow down and look for the clues. Horses are constantly trying to communicate with you by their often subtle actions to outright bold maneuvers, so pay attention to what is happening when you go ride and work around them. The more you can learn to pick up on, the more your polo will begin to improve.

Let's take it one step further with this fact about the power of the relationship between horse and player when it is done right. A top player has finesse. Finesse is that invisible timing that makes their game so smooth and seamless to watch. Why does it look so smooth? It looks so smooth, because the top player already knows what each horse they will get on is capable of and knows when not to ask them for a move that will produce negative results. They also know how willing each horse is to give their full potential and that is because of the relationship they have built with them in the hundreds of chukkers and single rides they have shared together. The horse is then utilized to its fullest and best potential for the good qualities the player knows they can perform well. These are details each top player has found out by lots of practice and riding with them before they get to the field for the actual tournament game, leaving nothing to chance. Those at the top understand fully what kind of relationship they can count on with each horse and therefore also know where is the best location to place them in their personal line up in a game to have the biggest positive effect for the team. That is such an advantage for a team and comes down to how well the player knows and relates with his or her horses. Yes, precision matters. That is what the relationship adds up to. The more you can fine tine it, the more precise you can be at all speeds. The average player or one who has not mastered their relationship with their horses will be like an airline pilot landing a 747 with no clue how long the runway below is before they begin their descent. That is where the relationship with your polo pony makes all the difference in the world.

That relationship is built in your daily interactions and practice with them before you get to the field. Being a great polo player is about precision and the ability to execute. It is in those hideously quick and surprise moments that it adds up to everything. The more precise you can be about what you feel is potentially coming from the horse underneath you, the closer you will be to kicking some serious ass on the polo field. The great player and horse combinations can move at top speeds in literally inches of other horses and plays that are developing depending on what is needed and the rider asks for, because they trust each other and know what to expect. Split second and precise decisions look seem less to the untrained eye and are what leave a new player in awe when they witness it. There is a real reason why top players can pull them off. They know the exact answer the horse will give and how much room the horse needs to perform it, before they ask for the move. Now that is a teammate that cannot be left out of the mix. Are you starting to see why the horse is your greatest teammate? Imagine that kind of maneuverability each and every time you enter the field. Now do you see why it is so important to get yourself in the saddle as often as possible? Wouldn't you like to have that kind of precision when you play?

That is the connection I am talking about that over rules all other sources of input when it comes to a polo player, including their human teammates. If the horse is on your side and in the game with you, there is no other feeling or power like it. There is no other teammate who can deliver this kind of benefit to your personal performance. That is why the relationship is so important. The horse is the absolute beginning and end to what you are able to do on the field. Without the backup of a good horse or one you are capable of managing well…you are nothing to the actual equation of the game that is playing out. That is why the horse is your absolute greatest teammate and the one you should give the most time to in practice. It will all add up to huge benefits over time.

When you recognize this fact, you will now be armed with serious potential. The relationship you will have with your horses is the most powerful partnership you will have in the sport of Polo and the key to opening the vault of extra power on the field. This is the one piece of knowledge as an aspiring polo player that will completely unlock those doors of improvement you couldn't seem to get through. Seeking knowledge and skills to improve this relationship and partnership will be one of the largest overall sources of benefits a player can discover. Then your personal rate of success is determined by what you the player are willing to put into the daily strategy of improving it. So get to the barn as often as you can, because your greatest teammates are waiting for you there with all of the answers. I encourage you to look for them, you will be amazed what is right under your nose and will help you go farther in the sport of Polo than you ever imagined ☺!

3

Step One to Steady Progress

Photo: Puma (aka: Reign Down Fire) Thoroughbred mare purchased off the racetrack, trained and played by Sunny.

Get ready, we are going to dive into a topic that is seriously hidden, but adds up to one the greatest sources of advancement a player can find. This is the one detail that never gets addressed properly until way after you have spent a bunch of time in Polo and are starting to wonder why your personal skills on the field aren't progressing as fast as you thought they would. This is the piece of advice and information about polo ponies that can add a tremendous amount of value to you the player and especially if you are the type of person who wants great results fast! Hopefully this will help explain why your Polo may not be progressing as fast as you would like and what you can do to start changing that. By the end of this chapter you should have a pretty good idea of the positive impact being able to answer this one question will mean to you...

"Do you know your style of horse?"

Being able to answer this question with a clear and defined answer means you know the best type of horse that adds the most to you personally as a player on the field. What I mean by player on the field is that you are actually participating in the "game that is happening and are a factor in the outcome" and not just a body on the trail ride. Did you know you could show up to Polo, participate in the game and never actually have an affect on the outcome of the game? Yes, that can happen and if if you are not aware of this one issue that may be holding you back, it could go on for years. That is a hard and expensive lesson in time to learn, but that is the lesson that will lead to the largest open door to improvement that there is in the sport. The horses you will play are the determining factor in your participation in a game or lack of and that is why it is so important to know the answer to that question. It will add to your ability to progress in the sport at a rapid and steady rate and that steady rate forward is what reaching the top of your potential is all about. Any time spent in the wrong direction means you are delaying your potential progress in game skills that you will need to learn eventually. You will be like the college student who graduates in 10 years instead of 4, because you had a lot of other things going on while trying to study. Additionally, if you are an amateur or professional player who intends to travel and will be playing borrowed horses, you will also do yourself a big favor to know exactly what type of horses best suit you and be sure and look for those in the horses that are offered. The more specific you can be to know what style of horse best suits you, the more time you will have to make great and effective plays on the field as opposed to fighting internal safety concerns when the games speeds up. Now, let's start uncovering the details to determine your own style of horse so you can start putting the information into action and speed up your rate of progress as a player.

Why does finding the right style horse matter?

First things first. Before we go into the actual clues to help you discover the right style horse for you, if you weren't able to answer the question right away, let me answer a burning question I am sure a few of you may have on the topic of "style of horse." I am sure there are a few of who you are thinking, "why does style matter?" Here is why. Doing well in the sport of Polo boils down to one single detail…the confidence you have with the horse you are on. That confidence is the basis for all you will attempt to try while on the field. No other way around it. Let me help you see this clearly.

What can you do as a polo player if you have confidence in your horse?

- ❖ You will be willing to take chances and engage in what you think is possible as the game unfolds.

- ❖ You will also be willing to push the boundaries of your skill level and go up against opponents that may outrank you.

- ❖ You will accelerate to plays that others will hesitate to push.

- ❖ You will push and hold lines when others have to waver, because of the change in speeds or tightness of company between horses.

- ❖ You will attempt daring shots and push for that small space between players where a ball is hiding.

- ❖ You will attempt to take on tougher opponents in defense to help your team.

- ❖ You will be willing to reach out for difficult shots that you don't normally take on all horses.

There are many more reasons to add to the list, but the underlying point to understand here is that confidence in your horse means that each chukker you will be entering and exiting plays with precision and an interest in stirring things up. When that happens…

- ❖ That means you are at your absolute best with nothing but the thoughts of the game and what you can do to have the greatest effect on the outcome of the game.

- ❖ You are 100% player…not just a rider in the pack of galloping horses.

- ❖ You are also able to focus on the strategy of the game and how to improve plays that you want to win.

- ❖ Each chukker that you have a horse that you are confident in, you will enjoy what you are doing and search for more to do in the chukker and that is where polo gets extremely addicting and your improvement potential is elevated to its highest level.

- ❖ That is also where you have set yourself up for the fastest rate of improvement potential as a player as well.

- ❖ The horses that give you confidence mean you can focus on the game and improving yourself individually.

A horse you are confident on is a tremendous gift to a polo player and especially one who wants to reach their full potential. With a horse you are confidant in you are also at your absolute best as a teammate and the most desirable when the invitations to play get passed out.

What is the game of Polo without solid confidence from the horse you are on? What actually happens on the field when you are not confident in the relationship you have with the horse you are on? Let me show you a few examples that you may be familiar with.

- ❖ You will not participate in anything, but what feels safe as the game whizzes by you.

- ❖ You might attempt to snatch a small bite of a play once in a while, but you will not be the "playmaker" or the one who determines the outcome of many plays.

- ❖ You will be more focused on just being able to get through the chukker or maybe even staying on the horse or keeping it under control as the game goes flying by you and you try to find the open space to hide out away from trouble.

- ❖ You will be severely limited and weak at best to try shots that are difficult. That means your team for that chukker is a little handicapped in your efforts as a teammate in offense.

- ❖ You will also be more focused on your horse, than the game. In fact, if things are really shaky between you and the horse, you will not be able to focus on making good plays at all in exchange for just being able to get around the field and not foul or get in someone's way.

❖ You will be stunting your personal progress in game strategy execution, because instead of getting to be a part of the action and having a potential effect on the outcome you have to keep your attention focused on where and how you will get to the play and will it be in the right timing.

There are many more examples to add to this list, but my point here is that you can not work on advancing your actual "game skills" (strategy, play execution, trying difficult new tasks that lead to improvement, etc.) when you are playing a horse you have no or little confidence in.

How did I learn this? I have ridden a lot of horses throughout my career and trust me when I say, they were not all ones that gave me confidence. In fact when I started out I rode a lot of monsters in horse suits that taught me a lot about the value of life and Polo. In the beginning of my career I had no budget for a made string so I had to find and make them myself. Cheap horses usually have a glitch unless you are lucky enough to find the diamonds in the rough… which I LOVE to do…and that is where the pursuit of knowledge and the discovery of horsemanship come in. It takes a whole lot of mistakes to find the right answers and the correct information and especially if you have an impossible dream you are after that there is no template for as I did. You have to search and search and keep trying different angles until you open the door that leads to the next level. That's also how I learned the best hiding places on a polo field to stay out of trouble until the horn blew ☺! If you do not have confidence in your horse you will also be less likely to push the gas pedal to full throttle and chase someone down or pass people when you get the ball. That means you will most likely have decided to take a defensive role that chukker, in an attempt to do something useful for the team. That means you will also most likely be playing with this mentality in your head …"I'll just get through this chukker." Any of this sound familiar? Those are just a few specific examples, so if they sound familiar, don't worry you are not alone. That kind of thinking goes on all around the world in the minds of many polo players at all levels of the sport. That is also why your personal relationship and your understanding of the important role a horse plays in your game and mindset as a player is so ultra important. That is a major part of what I wanted to explain in this first book on polo ponies. That adds up to a ton of hidden valuable details. That is why it is really important to slow down and start evaluating the style of horses you are playing and start looking for the ones that seem to bring out your best.

When you start to look at the horses you are playing in this way, aside from all the other details that go with them…and just singling this one item out for closer scrutiny…you will begin to see a pattern. There will be a pattern to the games that you do your best and which horses add to that success. There will also be a pattern to which horses add to the games that you feel the worst about in your performance. It may be one particular horse or it may be a couple of horses, but the one detail that will always stand out is in the confidence they give you or take away from you.

It's a fact. Not all horses give each player the same level of confidence. The style of horse is a bigger concept than you may realize and why I felt the need to include this topic as its own chapter in the first book on polo ponies, because I know how valuable this one concept truly is. As a polo player you should learn to ride as many types of horses as possible, but you should also be on the lookout along the way for that certain horse that really sets you above the rest in your confidence and willingness to dig deeper into the game as a potential threat on the field. That type of thinking sets you up for your greatest potential success in winning games, improving as a player and overall enjoyment of the sport on all levels.

An aspiring polo player can go nowhere in the sport without confidence. That is why finding the right style of horse for you individually is so ultra important. As a matter of fact, take a mental inventory of the horse or horses you are playing currently and answer this one question, this should help you see exactly what I am talking about.

"Which are your favorites to play?"

Now answer this question.

"Why?"

In every answer that just came out I bet there is a common theme and it starts with these words..."because when I play my favorite horse I can..." That is my point, the answer starts with "I can". When you are attempting to improve in Polo that means you need to step into uncharted territory in new skills, new speeds and new strategies and in order to be able to do it well, you need to be able to know you can count on the extremely powerful moving force underneath you no matter what. Any point where that connection between horse and rider becomes weakened due to a lack of confidence means you just lost some focus ability, because now that bit of focus needs to be shifted to self preservation or staying out of trouble in foul or safety potential. Sound familiar? That is why these small, but very effective insider details matter. The right style of horse means you can use all 7 minutes of a chukker to go get something done and the more you are able to do, the more confident you will become. It has a huge carry over in so many directions when you are playing the right type of horse and that is why you need to start paying attention to this one detail and start to answer the following question for each horse you are playing.

"Does this horse bring me confidence or some type of insecurities?"

When you take a minute to go through your entire string if you have multiple horses and answer that one question, you will start to see a pattern as to what type of horse you really get along best with. That is the answer we are after, but until you start looking at things this way you will just go along in your day to day practices and games without much shift in improvement and can't figure out why. This is how you start to identify the hidden details that add up to huge personal growth potential and they live in the confidence each horse will bring you or take away from you. Once you find the horses that rank at the bottom of your confidence list you can make some efforts by working with them more often to gain confidence or get to the answer that this horse is not for you and now understand the real reason why. This is a great start point to putting some good solutions for major improvement in motion. This will also be your chance at the fastest rate of growth potential if you really work on it consistently.

The clues you are looking for to discover your style of horse

The following information and advice is what I would consider to be essential for players to know about themselves. Get ready, you are in for some self-discovery coming soon, kind of like the Cosmopolitan surveys and quizzes only this time it is for horse info ☺! I am going to show you how to find the right horse for you as an individual on your own…without the heavy pressure of a horse trader full of potential benefits for you breathing down your neck for the sale, because his rig is pulling out in the morning. This is easy to assess if you have the right clues that can get you to the right answers. That is what I am about to line out for you as a guide you can always refer back to as your needs change and you need a reminder. Trust me when I say there are so many clues hidden in the horses you will ride and learning how to break them down to what is valuable and what is horrifically wrong for you will help speed up your advancement in the sport. Being confident that you are mounted correctly will also add to your overall enjoyment of the sport.

Also, please take note of this fact. The following specific details and clues I have included are also responsible for a big set of internal emotions within a polo player. Even though most of the time these emotions go unspoken they will set an immediate surge of energy through a player and that sets the entire tone for the chukker ahead. You might want to let that sink in for a minute, because it is for real and matters to you the player who wants to know what they can do to improve at a faster rate. And yes, this applies to both male and female players. The emotions of a player set the tone for the chukker to come and here is why. When you are intrigued and confident in a horse you just got on, you immediately set the mental bar that chukker on a task you want to achieve and what you are going to do. That is 100% forward progress in player growth potential to both a new player and to a seasoned player. Then there is the opposite. When you start the chukker with an immediate surge of "oh shit, I hope I don't run into someone or I hope I don't get run off with or I hope she doesn't start jumping when the pack goes by I better stay to the side this chukker etc."…you have just shifted from a player on the move up the ranks to a player who is just logging hours waiting until the real match of a horse shows up and you can re enter the game. Fact.

Each type of horse you will play will send you as the aspiring polo player in one of two directions…either forward to learn more about the game or stuck in place learning how to ride while the other 7 players are competing in the actual "game." To point out exactly what I am talking about I have made a list of some things you should take note of and see if they have effected you at some point or another. See which ones send your emotional triggers through the roof or to a really good place. These are some of the hidden factors that set you in motion to be confident with a horse or immediately throw you off your ability to focus on the game. This is the basis for discovering what is the right style of horse for you. Each player and what effects them is unique to their set of skills and personal comforts, so there is no wrong answer there is just the benefit to start discovering which style of horse sets you up for your greatest potential as a player. Learning to ride all kinds of horses easy or tough is a great part of becoming a top player, but it is the attention to detail about which horses really set you up for success that will escalate your rate of growth. Ok, here we go with the survey about style of horse.

See which ones grab your immediate attention…

- ❖ Do you like the head up in your face or down?
- ❖ Do you like a horse that pulls on you?
- ❖ Do you like a horse that goes on a loose rein?
- ❖ Do you like a tall horse?
- ❖ Do you like a short horse?
- ❖ Do you like a horse with a long stride?
- ❖ Do you like a horse with a short stride?
- ❖ Do you like a slender built horse?
- ❖ Do you prefer a wider, stout horse?
- ❖ Do you prefer a handy horse or a speed horse?
- ❖ Do you mind a horse that is hard to mount?
- ❖ Do you mind a horse that is hard to stop?
- ❖ Do you mind a horse that shakes its head?
- ❖ Do you mind a horse who is fresh as you start?
- ❖ Do you mind a horse that bucks on neck shots?

You will be doing yourself a huge favor if you start to look for certain small details like these that I have pointed out that either get you excited or freak you out. These small details can add up to a huge impact on the rate of your improvement and here is why. Why does all this matter to you? Let me start from the beginning and where every single play you will be willing to engage in on the polo field comes from. Let me help you see my point clearly with a small exercise. Put yourself on the last horse on the list and now in you're your mind, imagine heading out to play #One at full speed. How would you feel to pull the trigger on a neck shot that could win the game? Exactly. Your emotions will run high and probably instruct you to stay safe and maybe skip that option or attempt a half hearted swing without leaning out that ends up in the front legs. Yes, this is an extreme example, but the reality is this kind of decision to skip plays happens much more often than people realize. My point, no chance at executing anything precise or intentional, just the hope you get through the play. Those kind of missed plays add up over time.

If you really take a look at this list, it may seen kind of picky to the untrained horseman, but I am hear to tell you this is just the tip of the iceberg when it comes to the style of horse that will best suit you and where you are at in your personal riding skills. These are huge factors when it comes to what kind of confidence you will have on the polo field. If you will start to pay attention to which items listed above reflect the horse or horses you are playing that you feel your best on, you will start to see a pattern emerging.

> Learning the pattern to your success is what improving is all about.

It is also important to take note of the details listed above that really freak you out or send you into a large airplane turn scenario just waiting out the chukker. Both pieces of information matter and it is very important to know each of the patterns that apply to you personally. The good pattern and the "not for me" pattern. That is how you hit the target of the right horse and it takes time to discover it. When you start to pay attention to these kinds of details, you will also start to find a certain type stride a horse has that gives you the most confidence in your personal hitting skills. Over time when you begin to fine-tune yourself to what exactly gives you the player the most advantages, you will be setting yourself up for some serious improvement. That is why this is so important to start giving attention to these details, especially if you have never had this explained to you.

All top professionals know exactly what style of horse suits them best and they learned it through years of trying and playing all different kinds of horses as they progressed up the handicap scale, but what helped them reach the top is that special connection they have with the style of horse that best suits them and brings out their deepest level of confidence. There is no other substitute input for that.

Why does style matter to the new player?

To the new player this is step one to your future in Polo. Your improvement is all based on your confidence and feeling of safety when you first start. By going down the list I gave you in the previous pages, you can already start to see what bothers you and what you actually like about the physical traits of a horse and that is important to start paying attention to each time you ride. Finding the right style horse will also be a determining factor in your rate of improvement. If you want a fast rate of improvement you need to be able to stretch your limits of curiosity all the way when you are trying each new skill and in each practice game you sign up for. That is where style of horse comes in to play for you and big time. That is where these small clues that a horse will give you when you ride, like the previous list I laid out, can help you start to see what type of horse you do really well on.

If you are a new player, you should also always keep in mind that safety and confidence should always be your number one priority and should not be taken for granted. Finding the right style of horse for you individually means "you feel safe", not the seller that is trying to convince you it will all be ok, but your actual gut instincts. Trust them, they are there for a reason…your gut instincts that is. What do you feel safe to do on the field? Is the horse safe for you and the level of rider and player you are? Do you feel safe on the horse to run it full speed and be able to stop it anywhere on the field? Do you feel safe to leave the barn or does it have a major barn sour glitch that makes you nervous? Do you feel safe to hit all the shots on them or does the horse make you nervous when you really lean out because they may buck you off? These are all questions to ask yourself and especially if you are a new player. If the answer is no to any of those simple questions, you will be severely stunting your growth rate potential and overall enjoyment. You will ride many different types of horses when you start and they will all teach you something as you go, so I am not saying they are all bad, I am just saying to start paying attention to the ones that truly give you a feeling of safety and confidence as your main priority. Yes, your preference matters and it will continue to develop over time so pay attention to what you are feeling as you ride different horses. That list of small details is what you should start focusing on to help you find your perfect match. There are many more individual characteristics horses will have that can have an affect on a player, but that is a good start point to identifying some major ones to be on the lookout for that will separate your desires to play some horses over others. Finding the perfect match means you get to concentrate on learning the "actual game" and that is the fastest rate of growth you will be able to attach yourself to for sure. Finding the perfect match is also what will help you buy a whole lot less beer for your new friends at the polo club.

Why does style matter for the seasoned player?

It is even more important for you, the seasoned player, to know clearly what style horse best suits where you are at in your Polo career so far and here is why. Your confidence level will soar if you are riding horses that suit you and your style of play. Your personal style of play depends on what position you prefer to play and your rate of potential execution. You have been in the sport long enough that in order to improve you are looking for the extra edge and the really hidden details and a ton of them lie in the horses you are playing. Yes, you may think you got things covered because you have enough horses to cover all the chukkers of a game and a few bad chukkers really doesn't add up to much, but I have news for you. If you have a goal in the sport to reach your full potential you are wasting a whole lot of money owning any horse that is not bringing you enjoyment or confidence. Those two qualities are what will enhance your playing abilities and help you move up in the game faster than any other route. There is a real reason why and it goes like this. The more attention you are able to focus on the finer points of the game, strategy, team work, setting up plays to try and execute and scoring goals the more you will advance yourself as a player. Let me simplify it even more. It is counter productive during a game to have to give your focus to anything, but the task at hand of executing actual game strategies and individual plays associated with them. That is, if you mean to be the best player you can be.

If you are a seasoned player, by now you should know 100% what style of horse you do great on and which style of horse weakens your abilities on the field. Trust me when I say…it matters. You should also know that once you have that info, if you are serious about improving in the sport and have any type of goals you want to reach for yourself, you need to start managing your buying and selling habits to increase the number of horses that resemble pure confidence to you and find exit strategies for the ones who give you a bad reputation on the field in your inability to make plays consistently. Yes, when you cannot make plays on the field and are a seasoned player your teammates and the other team recognizes the impact. Spoken or unspoken…it occurs and is what is going on in the sideline chatter of your Handicap potential. Repeat this pattern of behavior too often and you will not be the subject of many team invitations or increases in Handicap anytime soon. How effective you are as an actual "player" and "team mate" comes down to how many chukkers in a game you can have an effect on the outcome of the chukker as opposed to just getting through it. Without working on this one detail to improve it over time until you get it right, no matter how small the moves may seem, you are literally putting a lid on your own potential.

Now that you know this, get busy on assessing your string and see what you discover. Each little detail you can improve on as a player counts, so just be patient and keep chipping away at it until you get to your best string. No 10 goal player made it happen in one season either, so take your time and make the best choices possible. If you will take a proactive look at the horses in your string and start creating strategies to improving the difficult ones or a potential exit strategy if you can not reach a solution you will end up with a better chukker or an open space for a new one that can enhance your game. This is the process all top players use and it is a continual one that happens each season as their needs change. It is the dedication to improving this area that over time will show itself in your abilities on the field and more of the chukkers that you can actually push the envelope in your skills. That is exactly where you want to be as a seasoned player who is able to gain ground at a steady rate. The biggest asset you have, lies in the horses you are playing and your ability to recognize which ones you do your best on. There is a reason the top players in the world will opt to double their best horse in the finals of an important tournament as opposed to playing a horse who is suited up, sound and ready to play. It's what they know that one special style of horse brings to their abilities…it matters.

Style can't matter right now because of budget?

What if your budget is really limited and you have to make do with what you have for now? Don't worry I got ya covered, been there too myself many times. For now you will have to make the best of the situation by working to improve the horses you have and learning all you can in the riding, fitness and schooling departments to find the extra detail that will bring out something better in the horse or horses that are troubling you currently. You will also want to start looking into the fitness, feed and routines of these horses to see if there is somewhere that a small tweak could help them in any one or all of those areas. It is in the search for solutions that we discover true horsemanship, so get to investigating what you think could help the situation and give it a shot.

Your situation now will also help you determine what kind of horse you would no longer enjoy to own when you have the chance to add new ones. All of it will pay off later as lessons you needed to learn to discover what you are absolutely NOT looking for in a horse in the future. That can be a very helpful tool that explains perfectly with a stamp on it what you "would like to have in your next horse" and what you "want to stay away from". Let's call the challenging horses you may own "clarifiers". They will help point out the style of horse you are looking for and how far out of the game you no longer want to be. Pay close attention to the traits that are most difficult for you as a player. That is what you will aim to stay away from in your new additions. That is where playing the wrong type of horse, although frustrating, is a great lesson to your future purchases. It will help you fine tune exactly what needs to go right when you are able to look for new additions. That is valuable information.

Being stuck in a budget crunch and having to play these type of horses until you can afford to add some new ones, can be a great mental gymnastics lesson as well, because they will challenge you in many ways in a game with your level of patience, your ability to think ahead, your ability to ride, your ability to develop a peripheral vision to avoid collisions, your sense of finesse and timing. Even though you may be stuck with a few of these type horses that are not best suited for you at the moment, they will also increase your ability to ride, because otherwise you will never see a ball in a game. You have to fight for every play that you actually want to get in and that means you will be challenged to find solutions so you can have an actual affect as a player. It is in the hunt for solutions that you discover the power of horsemanship.

Here is a personal example of how I learned some powerful information that truly helped me move up the ranks in my string building efforts. When I was climbing the ranks in tournament polo as a professional player, I had a pretty good string of competitive horses that I was pretty proud of, because I had made them all myself. But a few of them had an issue or two. At this particular place in my career, I was playing from 4-16 goal level polo professionally so the quality of horses was a topic I worked extremely hard at and especially given my limited budget. The type of horses I owned had to be able to play a large range in handicap levels so they needed to be pretty versatile as well. Ok, before I tell you the story let me make this one statement very clearly. When you step over the boards as a professional player who trains your own horses, the talk is over. It's time to see what you got in the horsepower department and there is no more room for b.s. ...you either get to the play or you don't. Enter Abilene, a beautiful thoroughbred mare to look at off the racetrack. Really fast, perfect size not too tall and not too short and really handy with some good speed and great to hit the ball on. One issue...for some reason she would every now and then when you checked her just hit a hard un-announced left turn. HARD TURN. I tried everything I knew to figure out why and what were the indicators for when that was going to happen as she just had everything a player could want...but this one issue. That's where budget comes in, I had none at the time to go get another one and she was quite sound to compete so I had to keep trying to figure out how I could make the best of the situation as she was really fun to play in spite of this one random incident. In fact, I used to love running down the field to goal on her, because she could pass or run with anyone and ran with great confidence to carry a ball on. Well here I go in the feature Sunday game one day with a full sidelines of people, party tents full of spectators and sponsors with a great announcer playing "Abilene". We were racing down the field and I was so excited to see a spot to get possession of the ball at a high rate of speed, as she was very fast. There we go, she managed to get so close to where I had aimed her as we headed for the center of the field at the boards that she literally went skimming on the tops of the boards as I attempted to fly by them all and fit through the small space that was left to steal the ball off the boards. With the party tents and side boards on my left and a herd of players coming up on my right side, I began to think of the one maneuver that could outfox the field and get me back to the middle of the field where I just knew she could blow by everyone and take me in a direct line to goal with this new shiny white ball I had just stolen. As I reached about mid-field right in front of the tents I knew I could out stop everyone so then came my big idea. I was going to pull the brakes, as I knew she could out stop almost anybody and let them all go by and play the ball back to the middle by myself. Then hit a haul ass run straight to goal…that was the big idea ☺! So as we all came flying to the absolute inside edge of the boards I pulled the brakes and she put on the best slide stop you've ever seen on grass and I was on a serious high how good this play was going to turn out…until she hung a HARD beautiful left turn so sharp and smooth that I never felt it coming and left her back flying high over the boards as she headed off the field the other direction. The play continued and there I was standing with my mallet in front of the tent, watching the play go down field without me and no horse in sight to get back on. I learned a lot that day. That is how you find out what you need to do without. I loved that mare, but realized two things that day in my horsemanship education. Two left turns could make a right turn and if I was serious about playing with the best players in the world and reaching the top I would need to make and play horses that did not have an un-announced glitch…it matters. That style of horse will not do for where I want to go in the sport. That is how you learn the best lessons and the ones that stick. You just have to go through them to find out what you cannot live with and what really does yourself some good when it comes to abilities on the field. True story lol.

A few more important details on style of horse

Remember this advice for future use. Your horse is who will deliver you to the play and who will provide you with the most options of what you can physically do when you get there. That is why style matters. You need to be confident what is coming from the horse and what you can expect from them at all times. If you are confident on the style of horse you are playing, its stride, its height and its attributes that give you a rush of positive energy you will reach your greatest potential as a polo player in the shortest amount of time. That is how you become the best polo player you can be. Finding your style of horse does not mean you can not play all types of horses, but what it does mean is that there is a big difference in the style of horse and how it affects your abilities in a game and let's face it, some horses you will hate the way they play even though they are very usable, but not intriguing and some horses you will absolutely beg to have another chukker on. Look at this concept I am explaining like dating. As you explore meeting people, there are immediate qualities you will be attracted to and immediate qualities that will turn you off. Your choice to proceed with an option that does not give you good vibes immediately, while trying to talk yourself into confidence because they are available and everyone else likes them will never produce the kind of results that you feel immediately in the right connection. That is what I am talking about here and the qualities in your horse you want to aim for and try to emulate. They matter and are the foundation of your ability to grow.

There is also a sheer sense of deep pride to look down your barn aisle at the string of horses you have when you are sure they represent your style of horse and an even greater sense of pride to pull them out of the stalls and love the way they look. Start looking at the strings of top players who you are inspired by and see if you can start detecting their style of horse. I guarantee you will find distinct similarities in their horses and the way they go and look. That is what I am talking about. It takes some time to find your own style, so be patient. You have to have ridden and played enough horses to really be able to see and feel a difference, but over time it can be such a huge pay off so you owe yourself some investigating. Get to it.

Getting to the correct answer for you personally will take a little investigating for those of you who are hearing this for the first time, so be willing to give it some time in the area of collecting info. But mark my words, if you do your homework in this area you will start to advance your polo at a much faster rate and here is the reason why. To be a better player than you were in the last game you have to be willing to do things you usually do not try. Playing the same style of horse that is causing you to lose time worrying when you could be progressing into new challenges is counterproductive to a player who is serious about improvement. Spend one chukker a game just hoping it goes by quick is one thing, but look at your entire string. If you are doing this in more than one chukker you need to take a serious look at what you are riding and why it needs to remain that way? Yes, this is how you start analyzing the hidden details that are holding you back. This is where you start doing the homework and coming up with the right answers that will lead you to a whole new level of possibilities. These are also the details that usually go unspoken to you unless it is so obvious or you have employed someone to give you professional advice. For most of the polo world…this is a learn as you go and your pocket book will allow situation. That is a large reason for this book and the topics in the book series as it unfolds. I want to give people resources to help them learn the lessons that are often the hardest to discover, but can be the most beneficial no matter how long you have been in the sport.

Are you one of the readers who are hearing about this for the first time and didn't know you could have a style of horse? Well I have good news for you, you can and it is a whole lot of fun when you get it right. When you start to consider what I am pointing out in this chapter your mind will begin to fill with thoughts of certain horses you have played who put a stamp on what I am saying in either direction based on what characteristics they had that you were attracted to or distracted you from playing well. Take some time to think through your current string or if you only own a horse or two so far, start putting this concept into your future horse buying habits and thoughts and you will save yourself a whole lot of money and time that otherwise would have been spent in the wrong direction. This one piece of advice can truly set you on the path to your fastest potential growth rate in improvement potential, so pay attention and get busy on finding your personal answers. They will pay off big time.

4

Are You Matched up Correctly?

Photo: Puma (aka: Reign Down Fire) TB mare purchased off the racetrack, trained and played by Sunny. This photo, Puma playing for Adolfo Cambiaso 40 Goal International Polo Club Palm Beach

Are you ready for some cold hard facts? This is the simplest issue to spot as a spectator and the hardest to know as the actual player. Yeah...its what's being talked about while you're playing and this particular detail matters if you want to improve. It's a fact whether it is verbalized or left in silence, it goes on and may be the culprit that is holding you back, but seems invisible to you. In polo the most important thing to be able to do is to be able to get to the desired destination on the field in exact timing and with precision if the situation changes. And trust me when I say, the situation will ALWAYS be changing and that is why unity and control of your horse is such a big issue to master. To be on the right skill level and type of horse for your riding and skill levels is the key factor to being able to maneuver through traffic with safety and execute plays effectively. It does not matter what you paid for the horse either...cheap or expensive. Over mounted and under-mounted happens in both directions of price. The result is the same...you are ineffective. To what degree you are ineffective depends on how bad the mismatch really is.

Some of the most beneficial information that you can search for in the sport of Polo, that has to do with polo ponies, is the matchup between player and horse and if it is correct. To be more specific here, I am talking about your actual skills and knowledge versus the talent, skills and training of the horse. This is an important equation to get right and means a lot to you the player who wants to improve. It is also not always easy to know and can be especially challenging if you are the do it yourself polo player who does not have access to a hired professional to point these kind of fine points out as you go. This next skill I will help you discover is one of the most beneficial tools to have as a player and one that you can use your entire polo career to reap some serious benefits that will keep you on track in the direction of improvement and good choices when it comes to the horses you are playing and purchasing. This is a really common situation that a lot of players will go through at various times in their polo experience. It goes like this. Everyone at some time or another plays with this one simple question running through his or her mind as the game rushes by you...

"Is it me... or the horse?"

Oh yes, it happens all over the world and you are not immune to the fun ☺! This is also what people are talking about while you play...the mismatch between the level of horse you are playing and your own personal skills. You have no idea how many people are playing with that one single question running through their mind and wish they could know the correct answer for sure. This topic is a huge concept to understand correctly about polo ponies and the effect the wrong ones can have on you in a game, so let me start from the beginning so you can get a clear picture of what is actually happening when you are in the middle of one of these dilemmas of a mismatch.

Learning to recognize when you are involved in a mismatch is one element to improving and learning to recognize when you are completely "out of your league" with the horses you are riding is a "must have" skill. This one small detail may help save your life and for sure your pocket book. This is also one of the most frustrating issues as a newer player, because the common advice you might hear from other people who have played the horse is that they love them, leaving you feeling very confused why you are getting the message you are and other people don't have an issue. There can be extremes when it comes to this topic so depending on which side of the equation you are going to relate to as I explain it, get ready to find out your own personal answers to know for sure as I explain a few hidden details to look for. Knowing what is going on with you and your horses and how you are actually matched up skill level wise takes a little investigation, but when you know what you are looking for as the clues you will be able to begin fixing your own situation faster than you thought was possible. And you will know how to answer that nagging question once and for all, so you can move forward.

Remember this fact about progress forward. You cannot properly address the problem that is holding you back, unless you know the real issue you are dealing with and that means cold hard facts. When you are able to have things broken down into small chunks of digestible info you can work on piece by piece, it all becomes very doable and kind of exciting to start addressing as you find a weak link. That is what I intend to give you one concept at a time when it comes to your horses or the ones you are playing. For each weak link you can improve on or replace with a stronger component, means you will have one new can of whoop ass to add to your game that you didn't have before. That is an extremely powerful weapon when it comes to improving in polo, because if you can conquer the horse element you will be way ahead of the pack in your competition. That is why I wanted to target the invisible details about Polo Ponies in this first book, because so many people are stuck with this nagging question and a lot of them are a little shy to start asking around…"is it me or the horses?" There is also the problem that the horse you just had trouble with is the expensive one you were just sold as a great horse and they assured you…"don't worry you'll grow into her."

The details we are going after in this chapter are slightly different than what we just covered in the importance of finding " your style of horse" that gives you confidence. What we are focused on here in this detail is the actual skill level of the horse or horses you are matched up with currently versus your own skill level as a player and rider. This is expert investigation, but have no fear it is only me and you here and my goal is to help you find your right answers so you can get to solid improvement and confidence you are at the correct answer. Look at what we are after like this. What are the likely results when you put a kid in an airplane cockpit with no flight experience and expect them to land the plane correctly and safely? What are the most likely results of driving a non-enhanced standard minivan in a Nascar race and expecting to win? That is what we are after here, your matchup with the level of horses you are playing. These are hard questions to answer at times, but until you start analyzing your own performance and in the area of hidden detail we are talking about here…your horse's abilities and how you match up with them in your skill level…you will go no where. You will make repeated mistakes in games and get some fun time spent in frustration or plateaus that seem unexplainable. Well no more being stuck. Learning to match yourself with horses properly is so beneficial and yet can be the hardest part to put together when you first start, because of how easy it is to buy and collect horses.

One more note before we get into what you are looking for. There is also the idea you don't actually want to hear the real answer that it may be you...lol ☺! Yes, we've all been there, so here is what I have learned along the way in my career about being matched up correctly and I hope it helps you answer your questions on this topic so you can get to a solution and move forward in your game asap.

What does it feel like in a mismatch?

Next I am going to explain the two actual terms "under mounted" and "over mounted" that I am going to use in this chapter and am talking about when it comes to determining if you are involved in a mismatch with the horse or horses you are having trouble with. Understanding these two concepts will also be the start point to answering the question…"Is it me…or the horse?" Each term has its own set of issues and potential negative side effects that will happen on the field, but the overall result is the same. You will be ineffective and perhaps in danger if the mismatch is really severe.

"Being under mounted is just as bad as being over mounted."

That statement holds true at all levels of the sport and at all Handicaps. It's a fact. There is a huge distinction between the player who is under mounted and the player who is over mounted, but the end result is the same. The player is ineffective due to the lack of horsemanship and it has an effect on the whole team in a tournament situation. It also has a major effect to your overall game enjoyment. To understand which category you fall in, "over mounted" or "under mounted" you have to first start determining what is the part of your game that you are frustrated with and then start breaking each answer down piece by piece until you get to the culprit. It may be just one of your chukkers in particular you are struggling with or it may be a few of them. If you want the easy quick answer, just ask a trusted player who is a bit better than you what is their opinion of the horse or horses in question and see what they say. It is usually very obvious to the spectator and especially the seasoned professional who watches you play on a regular basis, so get ready for some details you may not want to hear, but need to.

The mismatch in skills will manifest itself in this way. There will be plays you think you can make and you will find out the hard way your big idea has no follow through. Over time continuing to play a horse or horses that don't allow you to get to plays you see developing will start to wear on your confidence level. That can be a huge drain to a player's sense of potential, confidence and overall mindset. That is a dangerous area to stay in if you truly want to improve and think you can just wing it. Wing it when you have to, but get to work on solutions if you sense there is a potential problem. Give some thought to the next section as I will explain exactly what I mean when it comes to being over mounted and being under mounted, then see if either one applies to your current situation in any of your chukkers and the horses you are riding. This may be happening on one specific horse or an entire string.

OVER MOUNTED

The term "over mounted" generally refers to a player who is riding horses that are way above their personal riding skills level. Among the many causes of this situation, some of the most common and visible ones are too much speed for the rider to handle safely, too dangerous because of random behaviors the rider is unable to handle, and loss of control as the game heats up.

Negative side effects of being over mounted: The most obvious and hard to overcome mistake when you are over mounted is to fall into the trap of this common and well used phrase…"don't worry you will grow into her." Yes, there are certain situations where a player will be able to step up and grow into the skills of a top pony, but there are just as many negative situations where the horse is clearly a mismatch for the rider and is being allowed to stay in the string due to pure pressure from the seller or professional who arranged the situation. Yes, I did just say that. Often too many people are put in harms way by premature horse sales due to profit driven and expense related decisions over the potential client's needs. Don't be bullied, trust your gut instincts, it can save you in many ways. The other situation that causes a giant mismatch in a player being over mounted is a player who has purchased a really expensive horse that belongs in higher goal polo and has way too much speed for the player and where they are at in their own personal skills level. This can be a very dangerous combination, because the horse is able to execute maneuvers at a high rate of speed and a newer player who does not yet have the proper experience in finesse and timing is likely to send the horse into plays that they see, but with no real timing to execute properly, thus leaving opponents potentially vulnerable to being hit broadside or in front or behind the saddle on ride offs due to lack of experience, but ability to get there quickly. More precise example, try this one. Your 7-year-old son in a Ferrari with a full tank of gas. You can explain the instructions and consequences all you want, but at some point they will press the gas pedal and may have no clue of proper timing and distances or the power they are attached to. Yes, it's like that.

Another situation and common scenario of being over mounted is a newer player or rider attempting to "train as you go" a new high-powered thoroughbred prospect off the racetrack who has a lot of speed. Being over mounted in this scenario is potentially dangerous for everyone on the field, because a newer player needs time to learn the actual game themselves and when they are double tasking themselves with the training of a high powered horse with no steering wheel at the same time as themselves, the potential for a wreck is pretty high. This does not mean that it cannot be done, but what I aim to point out is a clear distinction in the potential dangers and explanations of what it means when you are over mounted and what to look out for. Those are a few of the most common examples to describe the situation, so hopefully you will start to see what I am attempting to point out that can truly affect your safety and progress if is left unaddressed. Without recognizing the potential setbacks, there is a high chance of injury to you - the other players on the field- and your horse – and the real danger is you will have no clue how far back a step you may be setting yourself up for until it happens. Remember, steps forward mean you recognize an issue and begin to look for better solutions. Being over mounted will also hold you back in improving your Polo and actual game skills because your main focus is now on the horse and maneuvering it safely through traffic as priority number one. That is a distinctly different priority than focusing on your strategy and execution of team work to accomplish a victory or best game performance.

Simplified... What does over mounted look and feel like? You will be in the seat of a Ferrari...bright red, fancy with all the options, looking great with the engine running and you flying down the freeway passing people looking HOT ☺! Only one issue...your hands are handcuffed behind your back when it comes to reaching the steering wheel to maneuver through traffic. Smile, because this might be a short and dangerous ride!

UNDER MOUNTED

The term under mounted generally refers to a player who is riding horses that are not suitable for the level of Polo they are playing. Among the many factors that can cause this scenario some very common and very visible ones are a lack of proper conditioning and care, visible lack of training, lack of actual talent, lack of speed or handiness and maneuverability in plays.

Negative effects of being under mounted: Why does being under-mounted matter to you? Let me explain. If you are a great player and you have or are playing mediocre horses you will ALWAYS be limiting your full potential and be stuck in a pattern of frustrating plateaus. The reason you will be stuck in frustrating plateaus is, because you are only as good as the horse underneath you. The horse is the extra edge that will put a stamp on the idea you have in your mind or the talents you have been practicing in your stick n ball sessions. At some point or another you will need to beat someone else to the ball to execute what you have in mind. That is where having the right style and quality of horse for your individual needs is absolutely key to being the best you can be. Did you know, you absolutely can show up to the game on time, have the horses all shined up, a fun team to play with and still never truly take a step forward in your playing career? If that is ok with you and you are only interested in having some fun and enjoying the action than no worries you can skip this section. But if you are a player who has actively been looking for a solid understanding of what it takes to improve in the sport of Polo, than you have to start giving time and attention to the hidden details that could be the potential cause of your stagnant growth rate. This area is a huge one to pay attention to. One of the most destructive things to being under mounted and not recognizing it for what it is, is that the player begins to tear apart their personal skills and begins to lose their confidence. You may want to re-read that last sentence once more. It is a big factor in a lot of un-necessary self-criticism that all players will get to experience at one point or another. When a player begins to see a pattern of mistakes and does not know the real cause, they begin to get frustrated and don't see the way forward, often because of this very hard to recognize or admit detail and are therefore stuck. This can be happening in one particular chukker or an entire string.

Now, let me clarify a few things when it comes to being under mounted that go without saying. If you are playing a green horse, well then it is already in your mind that you may be able to do less so you're not so hard on yourself. But when you are playing a horse or horses that you are familiar with and continually getting beat in games and plays you have to start analyzing why that is happening until you get to the real answer. Sometimes you will have outgrown horses that are in your string, but because they are so much fun to play and are sound you just keep playing them. There are times when you need to start adding better horses to replace the ones you may have outgrown. That will slow a player worse than almost any other factor, because if you don't see some inspiration that you are still improving it becomes a little frustrating and then starts the deterioration of your overall experience. Completely counterproductive to solid growth and very often the root of a stagnant growth rate, is the under mounted player who has not realized it. You can only go as far as your horse will let you or you are skilled to ask for. No matter how strong you are, it is your horse who has to run with the pack and be able to keep up when the play changes directions. You can muscle them all you want, but that is not what will help you the player improve. Improving your skills means you can actually participate in the "game" that is unfolding instead of just arriving to the scene of the crime at random intervals as your horse will allow you.

Simplified... You are going to get caught with your pants down. Fact. This may be in the way the horse's perform, are trained, or are conditioned, but will always be visible by the horse's inability to perform what the player is asking of them. The lack of performance is visible by difficulty maneuvering, handling speed changes or in a complete lack of speed compared to the other horses in that level of competition. This can happen when a player has jumped up in a level of tournament handicap level, but is still competing on horses that are best suited for slower or lower goal polo. This can also be extremely visible in the overall appearance, conditioning or quality of training in a player's horses. You are riding a bicycle on the freeway...good luck!

Benefits of being matched up correctly

The horses you will play determine your abilities as a teammate based on your fear of them or your confidence in them. Every single move you will make on the polo field has to do with the horse you are on and how much confidence you can draw from it. This is one of the main reasons why getting the right match up with your polo pony or ponies is so important to a polo player who wants to improve at any level of the sport. That is what the relationship is all about and your success is determined by how much you are willing to dedicate to learning about and growing the relationship in your daily interactions with your horses. Let me take it a step further to help you understand why I am putting such an emphasis on understanding the matchup up of you with your horses or the horses you are playing even if you don't happen to own them. Do you know that feeling you get, when you throw your leg over a horse and you know you can kick some serious ass for the entire chukker? That is the mindset I am talking about that is the best breeding ground for a great chance at improvement, enjoyment and wild ideas of the plays you will make or want to get into. It's like a garden with fertilized soil versus using a patch of dry desert sand trying to grow vegetables. Potential advancement in Polo is at its all time highest possibility when you get the horse factor matched up right. That is the ultimate breeding ground for success and actual high as a player and the most fun to experience. It does not mean you can't still play or you can not have a good time on a horse that is keeping you under or over mounted for your skill level or the amount of talent/training it has, but what I am saying is that you are the one holding yourself back by your own choices of what you are riding. That is a detail you can change. Even if you don't have the budget right now, the awareness of the fact will help you put in motion ideas to when and how you can replace the horse or how you can start to improve the horse with small adjustments and adding extra attention until you find a solution. That is how you take small steps each day to improve as a player.

Understanding the horse information is so ultra important to get it right, especially when it comes to knowing for sure if the horses you are playing are matched up correctly with your riding skill levels, your polo skill levels, fitness, feeding and training…it all matters and will show itself on the field under pressure. That is when you will see your personal answers displayed and if there exists a mismatch. When attempting to get the matchup correct, please keep in mind that each answer is unique to each horse you play. The reason I want you to understand this clearly is that it is often one of the slowest moving details to improve on and the greatest factor to a speedy rise in improvement when addressed correctly. Yes, that may seem confusing so let me simplify even more. When you have no clue if the horses you are riding are really well suited for you, you will spend a whole lot of time and money focused on the wrong details as to why your game is not improving at the rate you would like. You will try all kinds of solutions both that you found on your own for what you think is the problem holding you back and from the local players or pros that have suggested remedies to help you improve the situation. This can add up to a lot of wasted time and money if you are headed in the wrong and unfruitful direction. That is why it is so valuable to give some time and thought to assessing if you are matched up correctly with the horses you are playing in your skill levels versus theirs. It matters over time and as soon as you realize the facts, you can start to look for potential solutions so you can improve the situation. That is how you set yourself up for some serious advancement in the sport and it can be done on your own with small but significant steps like understanding this one valuable concept. That is the benefit to knowing and maintaining the matchup that is correct for you. You will be able to focus on "your game", "your skills as a player", "your forward progress" instead of just riding during the games and explaining to people and teammates what just happened and why you couldn't help.

5

How Strong is Your String?

Photo: 10 Goal player Gonzalito Pieres's Champion string being unloaded and lead to a US Open match.

Playing Polo on horses you love to play is the ultimate destination to strive for. Playing average horses, or horses that you are not so excited about or challenge you in the riding and fear departments can bring benefits of extra skills over time, but they will not accelerate your game skills like a great horse that you are confident in will. Think about this for a minute. When you watch the best players in the world compete, doesn't it seem like every chukker they kick serious ass and you wish you could play with that kind of motive? There is a real reason why they can do that. They have spent years fine tuning their strings and weeding out the horses that were holding them back. Yes, they work at it and that is what gives them the ability to kick ass every chukker. At that level they are only concentrated on the "player and game aspect" of their game. Yes, think about that for a second. When a player is only focused on "where you want to go, what you will do when you get there and how fast you can do it", that is 100% forward progress and that is where you want to be as an aspiring polo player as often as possible. This is the destination to strive for.

Now, let me explain how to put your own string in motion to reach its best potential like the top players. The type of horses that will set you on the path to the fastest rate of growth potential are the ones that when you leave the field, you can you say with no hesitation, "man, I wish I had ten like this one!" That is the type of horse that accelerates a player's growth potential at the fastest rate.

Why? Because that type of horse means you are 100% focused on the "player" and "game" aspects of learning the sport. By that I mean you are focused on where you want to go, what you will do when you get there and how fast you can do it. That is 100% forward progress towards improvement and the type of player that is most exciting to watch. Anything less means you are not able to grow as fast, because your ability to focus is now diluted with other stuff like trying to get the horse to maneuver and staying safe. You will lose the ability to work on strategy and play execution in place of being able to show up at the right time to the play. Understanding this concept is the beginning to serious improvement.

Your personal string strength can be explained very simply in an assessment strategy that I will explain to you now in the following pages. I am going to show you a simple ratio that will give you your own answer. Your overall string strength means your ability to focus on you the player and your actual game skills as opposed to just riding during the game. Yes, this is the core answer that will tell you how much you can actually get done on the field each time you go out. That is why knowing your own string strength matters. The problem with not knowing this one very helpful concept and knowing how to put it into use, is that you will continue to just go along and let those horse purchases pile up in your string without paying close attention to the end results that each horse is adding or subtracting from your overall ability to improve. That is where your wallet starts to disappear and your polo begins to take on a minimal to stagnant growth rate. The slower your growth rate potential the longer it will take you to get to the desired goal you may have in mind for yourself as a player. Take a minute to digest that…it matters.

Now, let's get started on a personal string improvement strategy I have included to help you assess your exact string strength and what to do with the information once you know what you have. There is no wrong or horrible answer to worry about, this is just a very useful tool that can help you to take a true evaluation of what you have in your horses that are contributing to your rate of improvement or a clear answer for a potential reason you are not improving as fast as you would like. This is an extremely valuable tool to use as you progress in the sport and your needs change as well. Always keep in mind, if you find out that your string is weaker than you had imagined it will take some time to improve it and this is the first step. The first step is always to know where the problems are so that you can then go about solving each one. That is where this extremely valuable assessment tool comes in to show you where you are at in your own string assembly. This is a great place to start if you are the player who really wants the insider answers to reaching the top and having a great string over time. If you are new to the sport and just beginning to purchase horses, than you will want to log this information as it will be extremely valuable as you start to acquire horses and want to be able to assess which are your best options of the horses offered for sale.

How to Evaluate Your String Strength

Let me help you see clearly how deep your current string is in horses that propel you forward at the fastest rate. This concept will help you see clearly what type of work you have to do to improve your string or how strong your string already is. What I am referring to when I say a strong string is not how strongly you feel about them or how many you have. What I am referring to is how well they play for you on the field that translates to your ability to cause damage and improve your own skills as a player. That is what will add up to you becoming the best player you would like to be and in the shortest amount of time. Here is the simplified way to get to an accurate answer in string assessment without someone trying to be nice and giving you a false answer that doesn't actually help your progress.

Answer the following questions and fill in the numbers below to see your personal string ratio and how you are doing in your own personal string strength.

1. How many of the total number of horses that you currently own, can you say without hesitation, that when you leave the field you go "man, I wish I had ten like this one?" _____

2. Total number of polo ponies you own _____

3. What is the difference (#2) - (#1) ? _____
(3 = number of horses that are so-so or you are not so excited about when you play or have issues that keep you from playing them)

Now fill in the blanks with your answers here:

Your Personal String Ratio: String Strength

#1 _____ (love to play)   vs.   #3_____ (so-so)

Did you come out with a greater number for #1 or was your greater number for #3? If you came out with a larger #1 than #3 you are doing great!!! Your string is dense in great horses for your personal needs and you are on the right track in your buying habits, so keep it up! Ok, now for the rest of you. Don't worry no one else is looking here and I won't tell if there is a huge #3!!! Let me let you in on a little secret about polo players and it is a VERY common one around the world due to how addicting the horse angle of the sport is and especially when it comes to collecting them. It is very common for players to have a larger #3…yes, that will be the most common result in the answer when you start asking fellow polo players those two simple questions. Most people do not look at it this way, but these are some of the most important facts I learned along the way in my career and the ones that truly made a difference to reaching the top of the sport and my best abilities on the field. Getting to the top takes honesty with what you have in your horses and how well you can perform on them. All top players know this fact about their horses being the base of their success on the field and that means more precisely, how many good ones they have that they can go all out on. And that it is what helps them excel and stay at the top. This strategy is also what top players execute each season in their daily efforts to get their strings to their best potential without even thinking about it. It is just part of the normal process of fine tuning the one element that they can not be without and that is great horses and a lot of them, no matter what the budget. That means they work at improving each horse they have until it is contributing positively to their career or they find an exit plan to replace them when possible, by letting the horse go to a player who does not require as much from them. All that matters to you, the person who just discovered this new information is that you now know the answer to your own assessment. That's all. If you came out with a larger #1 than #3 than it means you are doing great in string strength so far and congratulations! If you came out with a larger #3, then you just found out your string strength is not as strong as you thought and it is time to get to work on improving what you have or starting to make an exit strategy to replace the difficult ones as you can. Either way, you now have some seriously beneficial and solid information to go to work on that will take you to the next level in your own game.

When you start to look at your horses in this way, it will start to show you a very important element that all great players know is at the root of their success…string strength. Once you know your answer, you will have a distinct and correct impression of how crucial it is to make a great choice in your next purchase. Learning about this strategy to improving your string will help your bottom line in money flying out the window in the wrong direction as well, because the fact is, if you are unaware of the impact that adding one more average horse does to your current string strength than you are most likely still trying to put your make up on without a light in the bathroom. By taking this approach you will have some clear data why certain horses need to go and certain horses need to be kept. That is seriously valuable information that you can use to your benefit.

Now, what to do with the information

Ok, now that you have your personal string ratio results, you have some serious benefits to gain from it. If you scored a higher #1 than #3 than you are already doing your homework and can be confident that the buying and barn strategies you are executing are good ones so keep it up and always keep this strategic tool in mind if you find yourself slacking off in your progress on the field.

Now, if you are the reader who found yourself with a larger #3 than #1, it is time to get to work. This is what you can do to help improve your situation and overall string strength. Remember this is not going to happen overnight, so don't panic if you are already thinking how much it will cost to replace them all. That is not something to worry about right now. What is important to recognize is how to create the strategy that you can start implementing today that over time will get you to the right results and a great string that is really strong for you personally and the one that can actually help you grow to your full potential. That is the part that matters, so look at this like your blueprint to success. So here we go. Start by getting a piece of paper out and listing the horses that are in the #3 category by name and by ranking. Yes, give each horse a rank and from top to bottom, best to worst and a reason why next to them. Are they in the category because of repeated injury, are they there because they are tough to play, are they there because you are scared of them, are they there because of age, are they there because of a freaky quirk, are they there because of a health issue you can not solve…? Be sure and list them all, the horses and the main reason for each one being there. When you actually start to line out really basic and simple details on paper you will start to see a clear picture of what is holding you back and how solvable it is or isn't for each horse. You will also begin to see the work that needs to happen in order to improve your personal string. By listing it out you may also uncover a common issue among many horses, which is usually a repeated mistake. That is seriously valuable information, because that can be solved by stopping the behavior that is causing it. That can add tremendous value to your pocketbook in future mistakes you will now avoid repeating. Yes, it may look a little scary for a few of you who have never looked at your string in this way, but do not be intimidated just start to give this concept and strategy some consideration. Over time it will add tons of value to your overall string strength and your ability to manage it well and that is a tremendous asset all the way around.

Without taking the time to recognize this one small but very useful strategy, it is very easy to keep going to the barn and just seeing the group as a whole with no immediate solutions in mind. Over time, this will add up on your bottom line and most importantly your success as a player. If you want to be the best player possible, it is important to know where you can gain ground in improvements and your string strength is one of the most important areas to always be analyzing. Especially as you climb the ladder in handicap levels of tournaments and your horse needs change. Also, always remember this, just because a horse does not suit you personally does not mean that there is not someone out there with different needs who would love to have it.

What can you do with your new list of information? Start looking for solutions for each horse that doesn't light you up with excitement to play them or is unable to participate regularly because of one reason or another. By solutions I mean, can they be improved through some extra attention to details? Can they be improved through better fitness or feed? Can they be improved with some bridle changes? Could they be improved with some professional re-training? Do they need to be sold? Do they need to be retired? Start to look for the solution that will be beneficial to your string and the horse until you reach a solution that works. For each problem, there is always a solution so keep looking until you find it or ask a professional whom you respect what they would do in the situation with that particular horse if you can't find the answer.

With each potential solution you find for a horse on the list, you will have one more improved chukker or one less monthly maintenance expense.

Now do you see why this concept and tool can be so beneficial to you the player over time? This is how the best players in the world get to be the best. They work at each detail and string management, knowing exactly what they have in horses is how they do their best on the polo field. They know what they have in each chukker and that is because they spent the time behind the scenes working at it. Now that you have the professional insider info you too can get to work on what was holding you back that you may not have realized. It takes work and time implementing solutions to improve the horses in the #3 slot or replace them, but if you do start to implement this concept into your current routine of horse management you will be setting yourself up for some serious progress as a player.

Once you see what needs to be done it also becomes a lot easier to see the path forward in your own progress. Horse management done well will be one your biggest assets and especially knowing exactly what your own string looks like on paper. A strong string means, how well the horses in it suit your individual needs and what you are trying to accomplish. Using this one concept over time will really help you fine tune yourself to reaching your best potential string.

And here is fact number two. The more great horses you can own that will help you improve your ability to focus on the game, means the fastest route to improvement. Now do you see why finding out your personal string strength is so important to your success as a player?

Ps…don't worry if this has set you into a complete panic. This addiction you picked up will last a lifetime and the hunt for the next best horse is the most fun part! So enjoy the knowledge and just start implementing it as you can. That is part of the fun in becoming a great player and especially the constant hunt for the next best horse you can find. So make your list of #3's and why they are there and get to work, it might mean you are ready to go shopping for a new one ☺

6

Tips on Buying Polo Ponies

Photo: Devastation (aka: Blackie 1) TB Mare purchased off the racetrack, trained and played by Sunny.

Searching for that next horse to go into your string or if you are new to the sport, to get your string started is a fantastic adventure and one that can deliver amazing results if you know some guidelines upfront that will help send you in the right direction in each purchase. What I want to help you with here is the concept of always putting your personal needs and destination you would like to be in after the purchase at the top of your buying priorities. Yes, for each and every purchase you need to keep your personal needs in mind, because horses are so addicting that they will literally sneak up on you and before you know it, you own a bunch of them with no clue how that happened.

Part of what gets expensive in Polo is having to learn the knowledge by going through the mistakes. That is what takes time and each lesson usually means a horse you over spent for or didn't actually have the qualities you were looking for that you end up having to sell for a much lower price than you paid. That is what this chapter is all about. I want to help you skip those mistakes or at least reduce the likelihood of them happening anymore if you have already been down that road. The goal when buying polo ponies should always be to build the best string possible and one that is full of horses that you truly enjoy to play. Now, how do you stay away from the mistakes that will cost you the most in wasted time and money? That is what I am going to point out with the answers to a few very common purchasing questions one at a time. Each time you are in a position to buy a horse or need to make a decision that is a bit complicated is where there is the most risk for a quick and not so well thought out decision, which ultimately ends in a loss of money when the horse isn't what you hoped for. What I am going to touch on in this chapter are what I would say are the most common issues people run into when buying horses and the ones that usually add up to the biggest financial losses when purchases happen quickly and without a good opportunity to bounce ideas or questions off a professional for guidance.

Think of building your personal string like building your own personal army of tanks and weaponry. You want to make the absolute best purchase each time you commit and for a horse that represents your exact needs. Yes, you are in charge of recruiting your own army so make it a good one. It is important to take your time on each new purchase to make sure it is of the right caliber to your battle and one you feel 100% confidant on when you enter the field, that you are ready to do some serious damage. And I warn you now, Polo is some serious fun when you get your purchases right! The more specific you can be with a desired destination in mind that you would like to be in after you obtain the new addition, is the fastest way to building a great string. The following information is what a player can use to build the best string possible and to be able to understand why they are doing themselves a huge favor to seek out certain horses that hold the most value to their future success potential as a player. The use of these types of habits overtime will also keep your rate of growth potential at its highest level with each new addition that was the correct choice. Using these tips will also help you save some money and maintain the budget you had in mind by not having to replace horses that you bought by mistake or under pressure before you were 100 % confident they were the best choice for you personally.

Buying Green vs. Made Horses

One of the first areas a lot of players look to when they want to save some money is to buy a green horse or one who is ¾ made and make it themselves. Let me help you with that thinking in case you have had that thought or already have a few green ones in the barn you are working on and are an amateur player or rider. It may seem expensive to purchase a top made horse that you absolutely love, but what you are actually getting is exactly what you want and can be played today. That should cost a premium as the other two options, which are to either buy them green or breed them are products that will need to be assembled, tried and seasoned before you actually know what you have. And remember, for each year a horse needs to have to complete the training and seasoning process is a year worth of expenses. Now add those years up and see, depending on what level of care you provide in your own stabling arrangement expenses, what that might cost. Now add in the cost of a trainer or professional player who can train the horse unless you are planning on doing it yourself. That is where you have to know exactly what you are looking at and the correct way to evaluate a potential purchase and especially when it comes to buying green vs. made horses.

Now let me help you with some tips on that thinking and take it a step further, so you can see what is behind the curtains when you decide to buy a green horse. Each green horse you will buy needs to have training and time to become a made polo horse. There are several steps a horse must go through to complete the training process and then, when they do complete the training process, they will need a few seasons to become a fully "seasoned polo pony". What does that really mean to you the buyer who wants to end up with the right horses for you? A seasoned polo pony is one that you know what the consistency rate is when they play. Let that sink in for a second. Say what? Yes, a lot of knowing a polo pony's true value when you go to by it, is in knowing how consistent the horse is each time they go to the field for tournament polo. That is the information you need to know as a buyer and player who intends to move up the ranks. The horse that is absolutely consistent is the one you can set a pretty clear value on whether it is consistently terrible or consistently great. If you are not a professional horse trainer, than get yourself prepared for this small, but very important piece of information. You will not know the results in as far as the actual cost of this horse until many months down the road or potentially years. If you follow the correct steps and know the correct timing of when and how to push the horse, so that it absorbs training with confidence and is ready to be tested to its fullest capabilities with flying colors, you will have high odds of your horse being a good one, but the actual expenses that it will take to get it there will not be determined until the horse is fully "made". Your green horse will take time to get to where it can be of value as a new "made horse" in your string, so give that some serious thought no matter how cheap the horse is today as a prospect.

The idea in adding horses to your string is to create great ones that will be there for a long time, so that is why I am pointing out some of the unknowns you will be looking at if you choose to go the green horse route

Now, for those of you that are thinking you will train the horse yourself as you go there is nothing wrong with that thought and it can be done. But what you have to take into account is how this effects you "the player" while you are training your new horse. Yes, you will now be double tasked with two duties when you play. One is the training of the horse and the other is to take care that you do not put yourself in harms way while you show it the ropes of the game. That also means you will not be able to focus on "you the player" while you are playing this particular chukker. What does that mean to you the player who would like to improve your game skills? You are going to slow your rate of growth as an actual player down, because each and every chukker you will play the green horse needs to be for the good of that horse and that means you can not concentrate on "you the player". It is a mindset that needs to be separated when you enter the field to be able to achieve success in either direction. It is also very important that you recognize if you decide to go the route of making horses on your own, you will need to be able to switch yourself from "green horse riding mode" to "player mode" when you do hit the field for tournament polo. Trying to mix the two without a clear separation in your own mind when you are riding a made horse vs. a green horse will contribute to some **serious mystery plateaus** where you will think there is no way out. Riding green horses while trying to improve as a player also sets your hitting position in a way different place, that is centered more in the back of the horse for safety reasons where as a player who is working on themselves will be more forward seated to get the best hitting advantages. This one detail by itself is the cause of many amateur players getting extremely frustrated at the decline of hitting abilities with no clue that the simple fix is to adjust your riding position when you get on a made horse. What causes the setback in that situation? The reason is that you have combined two destinations for yourself in one type of horse that only has a limited capability to help you.

A top player is focused on their own game skills.

A top horse trainer is focused on helping the horse make its greatest moves and building confidence.

These are two distinctly different destinations that take specialized skills to do well.

Training your own horses is a fantastic experience, so my point to you the aspiring polo player, whether you are an amateur or a professional player is this. Just be educated what you are stepping into so that you can have the best results possible. Buying made means it is all about you and from chukker number one when you hit the field. Buying green means you will need to wait a long time until the game can be all about you. You will also need to be patient until the end of the training process to find out if this is a horse that is suitable for you that you truly enjoy to play. That is why the cost of a made horse may be worth it if your goal is to be the best player as soon as possible.

If you would like to by a green horse or a few prospects to give it a try then by all means get after it. That I have to say was one of the absolute most fun parts about the entire work behind achieving the goals I set out for myself in the sport of Polo. In order to reach what I was after I had to be able to compete with the best players in the world and they are riding machines! The hunt for the next horse and the adrenaline each new prospect gives you when you ride it and see the potential is a serious high and one that can be shared with your grooms and the team of people who share the same passion. It is a complete addiction and so much fun when you get it right. Just remember what I am pointing out here about timing, plan for plenty of it so the horse can progress at the correct rate and have the best ability to be a really good one. And, do not forget to **adjust your riding from "green horse style" to "player mode"** when you switch between green and made horses if they are comingled in your string, so that you can avoid mysterious hitting and playing plateaus that so many players get caught in. You will also want to give yourself the best chance of turning out a horse that is actually suitable to "you personally" and that comes in the buying of the actual prospect. Make sure when you decide on a prospect that it is the type of horse your personal skills are able to work with and that you are not intimidated by them. Buying over your head in the type of green horse you choose will set you up for sure early sale and a loss of money, not to mention potential injury. As your training skills progress you can add more difficulty, but if you are just starting out and really want to give it a try then do yourself a favor and pick a horse that you feel really confident with already. The horse you are confident in already, today as you look at it, is the one that you personally will be able to explore and push the most. Because remember, a green horse is going to enter the first few polo games like a giant Halloween haunted house and you have to be able to ride and guide them through it like no big deal so they can gain confidence. If you are already nervous about the horse just to go ride it, no way will you be able to show the horse confidence and that is what all green horses rely on to take steps into the unknown while learning to play Polo. I love the adventure of taking a horse from completely green to playing Polo, so I am not telling you not to do it. I am just trying to help you see what is involved so you can make the best choice for your Polo and enjoyment. One more note, if you choose to buy the wrong type of horse you may also be buying a lot of beer at practice until you get it right. One more way to look at it is this, if you have never trained a horse for polo and you would like to give it a try. Imagine what it must be like to buy a kit car or kit airplane that you assemble yourself. You will be responsible for putting the transmission and landing gear together so make sure to take your time and get it right if you want to have a safe and usable end product and one you can truly enjoy.

Look for horses that suit you vs. available

A lot of times horses are purchased because they are "available." That may sound funny, but is very common in the sport that players become interested to add a new horse to the string because someone lets them know of a horse that has just become available for sale. Then the fun begins, thinking how this horse could work for you the buyer. Instead of the other direction, which is buyer driven when you are ready to add some new value to the string. Trust me when I say a whole lot of money is wasted in the sport in this one small, but crucial detail and that is exactly why I am pointing it out to you now. Give this concept below some thought each time a horse is presented to you when you were not actually out on the hunt for one.

Visualize where you see this horse fitting in your string compared to the ones you already have.

Assess if this horse would fit at the top of your string or the bottom?

Then ask yourself, does this horse improve the line up I currently have when I make my horse list for the game or does it just provide me with another horse that is sound and can play?

Sounds simple, but you would be amazed how many horses get added to the string during a season without giving yourself small considerations that can add large benefits before you go ahead and buy it. If you can answer positively to those questions and especially "yes, this improves my horse line up" then you have a solid reason for proceeding, but if you can't answer yes than you will have a solid reason why it is ok to step back from the purchase and not have regrets that you missed out on the available horse. When you start to ask yourself questions about the benefits this horse will add to what you already have, then you will start to see a clear answer if this is a positive addition or if this is "just another horse in numbers." Remember each horse costs a monthly maintenance fee to have, so it is really important to make the best decisions possible each and every time you buy one.

You would be amazed how many people never give themselves "the buyer" a fair evaluation of the benefits they will receive and instead jump right into the trap of "its available, I better hurry before someone else grabs it and I miss out." Remember, always put yourself first and ask the question "what benefit will this horse add to my string."

If you are new to the sport and maybe a new rider as well, than it is always a good idea and very important if you want to hang on to your wallet a little longer, not to jump in too quick and purchase before you know exactly what style of horse you like and what level of horse you are looking for. That will add a tremendous amount of value when you do go to write the check on the next purchase or your first purchase.

I will also add that sometimes you get lucky and find great horses that become "available" when you were not looking, but always keep what I am saying in mind and make sure that they represent exactly what will suit your individual needs, or are an improvement to your string. Using this one concept will help reduce your potential financial losses that can start to pile up if you own a bunch of horses you are not truly enjoying to play and eventually need to replace them.

Buying a Made Horse with Previous Injuries

Now, here is a question so many people struggle with when it comes to buying polo ponies and trying to get to the right ones that will really suit them well. You go try a horse and it plays amazing and you are in Loooooove! Now comes the vet check. The owner assures you it is completely sound so you are not too worried, but you have the vet out anyway just to have a professional opinion and confidence in the price you will pay so that this horse will be with your for a while. Then misery comes when the vet report contains a list of previous injuries and now you are stuck with a dilemma…forget about the horse or try to negotiate the price?

How could this be or have happened? Setting aside the possibility that a true "horse trader" got a hold of you and tried to slip one by you, sometimes horses come from the race track and have injuries that are not visible to the untrained eye. Their old track injuries will become very visible when the vet does exploratory x-rays and in some cases goes as far as ultra sounds to discover old tendon tears and joint related chips etc. Yes, here is something to recognize before we continue. It is a fact that many horses that go through training for Polo all over the world do not always go through extensive vet checks when they are first purchased or raised as a prospect. It is a fact, as many trainers prefer to go with their own experiences and skip the vet's help due to cost or personal confidence. Now, that being said this is one of the reasons some great horses will be slow to sell, because at the point they are ready to sell is when the vet comes into the circle with lots of technology to spot old issues that may not have been flaring up while in training or completely missed by the trainer. It is at that point that most buyers become very nervous as to what to do, because here they have a great horse who is an unbelievable match to their playing style, but has these injuries. The horse seems fine and felt fine when you played it, but then you wonder how long will that last?

The question to answer is once again directed at you the buyer. What is your intent with this horse? Is this a horse you will need to rely on as a main part of your line up every game? Because if it is, you will do yourself a big favor to start out with a very sound one unless you have a great groom who knows how to manage the old injuries or you have the education and skills yourself.

Is this horse going to play high goal or low goal polo? This will help you determine how much stress will be getting put on this horse's legs when you play. There is a large difference in the amount of training and exercise that goes into a high goal horse vs. a low goal horse to get them to their highest potential in being ready for tournaments, so this should be a factor also. For example, a high goal horse in a top barn will go out for exercise twice a day for a minimum of six days of the week and that can add up over a long season of 4 months straight and the addition of tournament games every week. That takes a seriously skilled groom or owner to know how to manage injuries and get as many chukkers as possible out of the horse without harming them further or creating a potentially dangerous situation for both horse and rider.

You also have to ask what type of injury are we talking about? Is it a structural injury or is it cosmetic? A cosmetic eyesore to look at that has no effect on the structural soundness of a horse can often be nothing more than a great bargaining tool to negotiate the price down. But, you have to know the difference or be able to have a reliable professional to discuss it with for the knowledge and correct answer. A horse with a major structural injury such as a severely torn suspensory or bone fracture in the lower extremities is a very risky place to start if you are counting on this horse to run down the field at full speed and be able to handle all kinds of terrains in field conditions and not have the chance to reinjure or worse, break down completely. Some structural injuries can be managed, but you have to know exactly the extent of damage and make sure that what you will ask the horse to do physically will not overburden there limits. That usually means a step down in the level of Polo they are capable of playing or the caliber of player that is playing them, so they are less stressed as well as the addition of major follow through dedication in physical therapy and monitoring during the season to maintain their health and wellness. This also means you need to have a solid understanding of how a proper fitness program will help maintain the horse properly. Many older horses who have old injuries that are set in the healing process are great starter horses for new players, because they have so much experience under their belt that a young horse does not yet have. Almost all horses will having something that pops out on a vet check, the question becomes how severe is it and what is the danger to the horse or yourself that is a potential risk to be aware of? That is how you start to get to the correct answer or whether or not to proceed with the purchase.

If this is a circumstance that happens to you here are a few pieces of advice to keep in mind when making the decision to proceed or pass all together. These are just guidelines and there are literally thousands more details you can use to help make the best decisions, but this should give you a basic idea of things to look out for and take into consideration. My goal is to help you get to the right horse purchases and some of the decisions you need to make to get there are sometimes very complicated. Hopefully these few tips will help you get to the decision that is right for you as well as give you an idea of the right questions to ask when this situation presents itself.

1. Is the old injury in a location or was so severe that the horse could actually break down when running or turning? This is something to stay away from, as it can be fatal to both you and the

horse if the horse goes down while you are playing. This horse may need to be retired. Sometimes these type issues have been previously hidden with veterinarian prescribed "numbing" or "nerving" procedures, so it is very important to know what exactly is the extent of a major structural injury to the legs front or back and do not be intimidated to ask the hard questions.

2. Is the injury a supporting structure to one or more of the horse's legs or a cosmetic blemish in the skin or hide? If the injury is a cosmetic blemish, such as an old wire scar across the chest or hindquarter that effects no muscle or ligament movements then you are dealing with a potential price negotiation for the defect. Sometimes horses will have previous injuries that do not effect their actual movement or soundness, such as what I mentioned above or minor splints that are just noticeable when you look the horse over as a blemish. It is important to be able to know the answer to this question, before making your decision.

3. Is the injury fully healed? This is important to know, because if the injury is not completely healed and is still in the healing process you will need to give the horse time off to recover fully so that the injury does not reoccur. This effects when you can actually have the horse in your

string and available to play. This also effects your cost as you will need to add expenses turning the horse out while they heal or having them in a stall if that is what is required in the rehab process. Time to recover costs money, so this needs to be considered as well as the healing recovery potential depending on how severe the injury was in the first place. Just because an injury has had the immediate inflammation drawn out through the correct rehab procedures does not mean that the injury is completely healed and the horse is ready to add the stress of hard work yet. This can be a huge and costly mistake if you don't know the correct answer.

Those three examples and tips can help clear up a lot of confusion and here is one more. Always ask the veterinarian what is your worst-case scenario? Don't assume you know by the seller's reassurance, go ahead and ask the vet so you will have an ample amount of input before you make the decision. You may also want to consult a local professional whom you value the opinion of and knows what type of player you are, what they would do. The more input you can get, the more of an informed decision you can make and that can seriously help in the complicated decisions that will arise when buying a horse with previous injuries.

Keep this advice in mind as well. Most older polo horses will carry some type of old injury or visible wear and tear somewhere on their legs or body. That is quite common due to the amount of work that goes into playing and training to get ready to play as well as the level of barn care a horse receives or does not receive while in work. Just because a horse has previous injuries does not mean it can not play polo, it just means you need to educate yourself on what that injury means to the safety and soundness potential of the horse and how that will work in your string. Remember, for each time the horse needs rehab to recover from the injury means you will be short a chukker, but continuing to carry the monthly barn expense. So that is why it will really help you if you know what you are doing when you start buying or adding horses to your string and especially the ones with previous injuries. Each horse matters and each time you get presented with a complicated situation, like the horse with previous injuries, you will do yourself a large favor to ask as many questions as possible and do not be intimidated by sellers or vets who may attempt to pressure you one way or the other. Always use your gut instinct and weigh the information before making the decision. The point is to ask a lot of questions until you feel like you have enough information to make the right choice for you and your goal of adding great horses of value to your string that are safe to play.

Aim for the Top in Your Purchases

Ok, this section is for the player who wants to hit the top of their potential as fast as possible. Having great horses is the key to achieving the greatest amount of growth in the shortest amount of time. Fact. This part is for the person who already owns a horse or two and wants to take the next step in their game as fast as possible. If you are new to Polo, then please log this information, as it will be extremely beneficial for you when it is time to start buying polo ponies. Becoming the best player you can be means you will need to be able to give 100% concentration to the game when you play and not your horses and that takes a buying formula to be able to get to. This is the buying formula that will help you get to that equation, where you are advancing at the fastest rate possible. Improving and building your string means you should be looking to match or outdo your top 1-3 horses in your current string in each next addition that you set out to purchase. Using this one tip can help accelerate your growth potential as a player in a huge way. Here is why. Each new chukker you can add to a game that you are only focused on your game and doing your absolute best in strategy and play execution means you have one new chukker to work on "you" the actual player and your game skills instead of just trying to manage the horse and get through the chukker. Imagine being able to play all four or six chukkers in a game on horses like your top 1-3? That is what you should be aiming for and that is exactly what I am trying to describe that is so important to try and emulate in the next horse purchases. It makes a huge difference over time if you have 5 out of six chukkers where you can kick some serious ass, as opposed to having 3 of your six chukkers where you are ready for business and the other 3 chukkers you just try and do your best to mark a man or be useful where and when the horse will allow you to get there. See my point? Over time these games add up and that is where a player can gain serious ground if they will help themselves in their buying habits. Yes, this takes time to implement, but it is a concept that will help elevate you faster than any other single component you can grab a hold of. This is the one concept and formula to work on and master. It will add huge benefits over time. The situation is even more meaningful in 4 chukker Polo, because you only have four chances to overcome the other team and one additional great horse means a lot in your performance potential as a player.

Remember, part of being a great player is what you can actually pull off when you are in the game, not just showing up. So, the way to get more of those kinds of chukkers in your string is to set a standard when you go to buy that goes like this. The new purchase has to be at least as good or better than one of the horses that hold the top three spots in your string. Use those 1-3 horses as your personal measuring stick to hold up against the potential new purchase and really analyze where it will potentially fit in against them. If you start to add this to your buying habits, you will be setting yourself up for a larger and faster rate of success in achieving your personal goals in the sport as a player. This is a fact that will add tremendous value to your overall experience in Polo and to saving money by knowing exactly which horses will help take you to the next level.

Buying Tips for the New Player

Now, if you are new to polo and only own one horse so far or even newer and you are getting ready to purchase your first horse this section is just for you. Here are a few tips and questions you will want to keep in mind so that your first purchases are right on target and ones that will give you the most enjoyment when you start.

Here are a few questions to keep in mind and ask yourself about the horse you have tried or are planning to try:

1. "Do I feel confident on this horse?" It is really important that your first horse purchase gives you a lot of confidence. Confidence will allow you to explore the sport at a much safer and faster rate. If you settle for less and let yourself get pressured into a quick purchase, you will be a little insecure to go practice and ride if the horse gives you lots of questions and doubts when you get on it. So do yourself a favor and wait until you can answer yes to that one question and you will save yourself a lot of frustration in so-so chukkers to come and potential money lost.

2. "Do I feel 100% safe when I ride and play this horse?" Notice I said ask yourself both about "riding" and "playing"? This is a huge point to make, because some

polo ponies are great to play and some of them are not the best to go riding on for one reason or another. It is very important if you are the new player that you find a horse that is safe to actually ride on (away from actually playing a game), because you will want to be able to spend as much time in the saddle as possible to improve. That means you need to be able to go to the barn and head out to the track or stick n ball field on your own with no worries of barn sour or potential dangerous behaviors that will get you hurt or knock your confidence. For you, the key to your quickest rate of growth is riding a horse that gives you 100% confidence and that is why you have to be really diligent when a horse becomes available to ask the right questions. If you go ahead and buy a horse that plays great, but is kind of scary to ride you have just cut your growth rate potential in half. If you go ahead and buy a horse that rides great, but scares you when you play it, you have just done the same thing…cut your potential growth rate in half. The horse that you can do both on (ride and play) means you can have double the capability of riding time and practicing with confidence. Following this one tip means that's you can confidently take advantage of both options to improve yourself each time you choose to practice or go to ride.

Confidence builds a solid foundation especially if you are a new rider as well as player coming into the sport. Confident is where you want to be when you start and when you say yes to the first horse purchase or two. This first and second horse purchase are huge factors that will determine a lot about your future in Polo, so make sure and assess these factors I have pointed out when someone hits you up with a potential horse purchase that is available. Please also note, it is not necessary to be John Wayne and cowboy up on your first horse purchase on a wild bronco that scares you. Wait for the one that you feel great on. It will be well worth the wait.

Remember this one huge factor regarding expenditures in Polo. Buying is one cost and maintaining each horse is another cost. That is why making sure you have the right horse can save you a whole lot of money over time.

Here is another very common question and line of thinking that a lot of new players have when it comes to buying their first horse or horses. Get ready to cross this bridge when you go to buy that will send you into a serious dilemma. Should I try to buy all young horses so they can be with me a while and will be strong and fast or should I be open to buying older horses? The first horse purchases should be about horses that give you, the new player, the most confidence. Young horses may still need time to mature into the end result of a seasoned made horse and can change a little as you go depending on their environment and input. The more Polo experience and specifically tournament polo experience a horse has, the easier it will be for you to concentrate on learning the game with. Older horses are fantastic starter horses as they know the game and can help you learn the game in ways an inexperienced horse can't match. Older horses can also often be purchased at discounted prices because of their age or old injuries. Always be open to trying older horses that have a tremendous amount of experience, because if you purchase them right they are usually worth their weight in Gold and can be sold to another new player at a decent price when you outgrow them. This helps you recover your initial investment as well when you are ready to move up in your skills and purchase additional horses. One thing to keep in mind also. If you are new to the sport one of the absolute best bargains you can find is an older horse, with a ton of experience who may have an old injury or two that no longer affects their performance. These type of horses can almost always be found at a reduced price near the end of the season when players are getting ready to turn their horses out after a season or travel to the next club as a professional.

Another tip to keep in mind is this one if you have been taking lessons for a while and now are ready to buy a horse. Make sure that the horse you purchase is at least as good or better than the favorite horse or two you have been taking lessons on or have been renting. That will be your first target to hit in your early purchases. If you will start out buying horses with that thought pattern you will find your enjoyment level will stay at the highest rate and that is where Polo takes over your life and the greatest new lifestyle will set in permanently ☺!

A few more points to keep in mind

My whole point in this chapter is to help you "the buyer" to start training yourself, through each example I have given, to always **keep your end result needs in mind** as you go through the buying process. Have a clear destination in mind what it is you are looking for and always assess how the horse meets those criteria in order to improve your personal buying skills and overall benefits you will receive as the player. It is extremely easy to get caught up in the romance of a new horse coming into the string like a first date, so make sure you give it time and considerations to what you are trying to accomplish before you hand over the cash.

The other really important tip that can help you big time if you are headed towards the purchase, but for some reason still have some hesitations. **Create an exit strategy with the seller** in case the horse does not meet your expectations for one reason or another. Eager and reputable sellers are often very willing to work something out, such as take the horse and re-sell them or replace them with a different one, or attempt to help you resolve the actual glitch that could pop up, but you will never know unless you ask before you commit. This is especially necessary if you are buying horses that will need to be imported. Without a clear exit strategy you may be out the entire plane ticket, horse and expenses in between, so it is 100% valuable to ask the seller, what happens if the horse does not work out for me once I get it home or the wrong one shows up at the import barn and is not the one I bought? You may be laughing, but that does actually happen. I know new players who have purchased horses and upon picking them up at the airport quarantine find out they have 16 horses they have never even seen before and were left with the entire bill, no resolution and even worse were not the level of horses they could really even use in their string. Without giving yourself the buyer some room to know your worst-case scenario before you finalize the deal you may be left with a large doubt that could have been addressed had you known to ask. This one tip can save a lot of headaches and a lot of cash, so hopefully you will always keep this in mind where it can help you.

One more point to make about older horses. Did you know that there are a lot of horses competing in the US Open level of Polo that are often times over 15 years old and even a few in their 20's? Fact. Some of the best horses in the world only start to get noticed at about 10-15 years old when their best qualities as the seasoned and mature horse they have become start to shine. Just a little factor to keep in mind.

7

Tips on Buying Prospects

*Photo: Prada, purchased as a yearling prospect at auction, trained and played by Sunny. Best Playing Pony winner, played up to US Open level.

How to Choose the Right Prospect for You

This is where the whole process and potential success of a polo pony begins. What kind of talent are you choosing to start with? The choice you make will determine where your horse is most likely to end up in the level of polo it will play, the abilities it will be able to develop and the actual end point sale price if you are the trainer or breeder. Choosing the right prospect means you need to make the right choice for your training and riding skills as well, not just what the horse is capable of. If there is a giant mismatch in the type of horse you have chosen versus your own training skills, you will be asking for trouble in a quality end result product unless you are willing to grow your knowledge and abilities or look for professional help to guide you in the process when you hit a snag. Example: if you buy a fantastic looking two year old off the race track that is full of energy and you are a timid rider who prefers the safety and security of a ranch broke horse to work with, you have already saddled yourself with difficult odds to get the job done right. Does not mean you will not get to a result, but pay attention to your skills when you choose the horse and what is your intended result in the "finished product". Make sure your choice of prospect is a horse you are capable of managing and riding, because making a polo horse takes daily riding and if you are afraid of the prospect you have chosen you will be very likely to find all kinds of excuses why today is not the best day for training. That is how horses get to be 7 or 8 years old and you still own them as "green horses" that are not yet finished.

It is also important to try and answer the following questions when you set out to buy a prospect, because the answers truly matter to what level of success you will reach.

- ❖ Is this a project horse for you to enjoy?
- ❖ Is this a prospect you intend to make and sell at a high return and profit?
- ❖ Is this a prospect that will go into your own personal string?
- ❖ Is this a prospect you are aiming at selling to high goal or low goal?
- ❖ Is this a prospect you are going to sell to a patron or a professional?
- ❖ Is this a horse you intend to finance for a long time or a prospect you want to flip rather quickly as a started horse? This is a huge point to define…before…you pull the trigger and write the check. This will tell you a lot about the type of horse you are best suited to start with for your intended results if timing is an issue to consider.

There is a real reason why you will want to know the answers to the above questions. You will want to actually compare the horse you are looking at with the question that applies to you and see how they measure up in the possibility to meet your criteria.

Horses can get really expensive if you are unsure of what you are after. This process and list of questions will help you get started to identifying the correct horses for you personally and your desired results. This will also help you be able to answer "no" this horse is not likely to meet my needs as well. This is a valuable tool to put in place as a buying habit when you go looking. Ok, let me just state another fact. Sometimes you just see one and have to buy it. Absolutely gotta have it and there you go, you own it ☺! I have been there done that many times! Then the fun begins discovering what the horse can do and then you decide what the rest of the answers will be as you ride it and you become aware of the possibilities and shortfalls. Ok, yes…that is VERY common, because as I said before, horses are addicting and buying them is just as addicting and so much darn fun! My point is this. There is no wrong answer to what you buy unless you have an exact result you want to get to. That is my point.

Training horses is a complete blast and a passion that is shared among players, grooms and horse trainers all over the world. Each new horse is an adventure and the results with each new prospect will be known when you get there. But for the person who wants to reach a desired result and has a timeframe in mind of when you want to get there, then you will do yourself a giant favor to pay close attention to what you are selecting when you start out and if it can match up to your intended timeframe and sale results. Yes, your success starts in what type of horse you choose and that will determine your odds of succeeding right out of the gate. If you want great results more than once, buying the right prospect that matches the timeframe you have in mind to complete the process and matches your personal training skills is where you set yourself up for the greatest chances at success no matter if you are an amateur or professional. Oh and one more warning about success with choosing prospects. There are horses who will make themselves and trick you into thinking you are special, so pay attention to the processes you can repeat with success and be thankful when you do get a one in a million horse.

Know the end result you are looking for before you go shopping

When you decide you are going to go buy a prospect, make sure to determine first, exactly what type of horse you are looking for in a finished product and work backwards from there. When you start to use this as a buying concept, you will start to hit your target in great horses faster than you know. This buying habit will also help you cut out owning too many of the "in between horses", the ones that play, but are not really what you were looking for. The more precise you can be about what it is you are looking for in a prospect, meaning "end results desired" such as level of polo to play, who it is intended for, what time frame it needs to be made in and what price range you intend to sell it for, the sooner you can get to a great prospect choice that will have the best chance of reaching your goals. This may seem tedious, but trust me when I say it is a great buying practice when you can get in the habit of looking at horses with your end result in mind. Then ask yourself do they measure up if you were the intended "future buyer"? Does is it have great legs, does it have great conformation, does it have previous injuries, does it have barn glitches such as cribbing and pulling back at the tie rails? Whatever you start with is what you will have when you are done as well, unless you are a great trainer and can remove the issues that made it cheap as a prospect. Think about that for a moment. Therefore, if you are starting with a prospect that has previous injuries, it does not mean that the horse will not play polo, but it does mean you have already saddled yourself with some serious baggage if you intend to sell them at a high price when your training is all through. Giving time to choosing the right prospect is everything when it comes to reaching your best chance at a great horse.

Choosing the right prospect also makes a huge difference if the horse is intended for your personal string. This has to do with what I call finding your style of horse that I covered in the earlier chapters, so for now just know that the prospect you choose should be in line with the style of horse that is at the top of your string right now. Think of the new prospect as a fresh piece of clay …do they fit the mold of your best two to three horses or are they way off? If you can look at buying prospects in this precise way you will build a very successful and strong string of horses for yourself over time. Buying a different type horse that will ultimately play is not wrong, but if you are going to spend the time and money attempting to "do it yourself" don't you want to try and reach your new next best horse as the bar you set when you start out? This is the one tip that can help you reach that as your goal and that is what I want to help you do, so you can have more great horses that will suit you personally.

Choose a horse that matches your skill level

This is a very important tip to pay attention to and especially if you like the size of your current wallet. Take the time to select the best possible prospect that will be a good match for your current equestrian and polo skills. Let me explain a little further why it is so important to choose a horse that you are a good match with. Choosing a horse that is way above your own riding and horsemanship level is a potential disaster in motion unless you intend to spend every single day in pursuit of improving yourself and getting help when necessary to avoid getting either one of you injured. If you will be honest with yourself about your own riding and skills level in Polo and how that will match up with the potential purchase, you will save yourself some serious frustration and potential loss of money. Remember this fact. A prospect will become the greatest polo pony possible if it can progress through the steps of training and be able to gain confidence and trust in each step. That means you need to be able to deliver the lessons with confidence yourself in order to drown out any insecurities the horse may have that will present themselves as you go. Any setbacks in trust or confidence that the horse finds an out for, meaning you can't solve or decide to skip all together means one more question and doubt the horse will always carry in their mind about fully committing to what you are asking. This is a major and underlying reason for horses who end up playing, but have a small issue with committing themselves entirely to what you are asking. This means in simple terms, the horse you end up with may have some "clutch driven moves" to force them through plays instead of clean and dramatic desire to do exactly what you ask when you ask for it. Yes, it carries over to your end result handle capability and trust that a horse is willing to give you on the field in tight and tricky situations and especially manifests itself at speed. When you get the matchup correct between your skills and the type of horse you have chosen, you are setting yourself up for the potential at a very successful finished product and potential profitable sale when you are done. The opposite of that, when you get the matchup wrong and rush to purchase one before assessing if you can actually handle the level of horse it is, will send you into some seriously frustrating situations and the eventual need for professional help or the sale of the horse, because it is too dangerous for your skills level and what it is being introduced to that you can not explain properly.

Make no mistake, each new horse you take on will teach you about training horses and that is the process to becoming a great trainer. But if you are truly seeking to get to a quality "made horse" at the end of your journey together, than take the time to pay attention to the matchup in your skill levels versus the type of horse you are choosing. With each correct choice, you are setting yourself up to advance in horsemanship with a solid foundation that will carry over additionally to your polo skills. Here is a side effect of great choices that most people don't recognize as well. With each time you successfully train a horse for Polo, you will also be giving yourself confidence (solid foundation) how to solve issues as you are riding and playing. This can add a great amount of extra hidden skills and extra confidence in playing when you hit a snag with a horse. Your confidence in training will kick in and you may have a much greater list of options to fix the problem on the fly in a game, than you did before. This is a tremendously valuable skill if you play unknown horses in your travels or are a professional who plays horses from a team string that are not yours. Keep this tip in mind when you head out to hunt for prospects and you will have a much greater chance at coming out with a solid product after your investment of time and money.

How important is conformation in the new prospect?

Prospects with great conformation usually demand higher purchase prices, where as a horse with average confirmation usually can be bought at a lesser price, because they are not so glitzy to the eye at first. This is a huge section of importance to pay attention to, as you progress in your horse training skills, so be willing to give some time to learning through your good and bad choices. This is where you get to start with a seriously athletic choice or one that will need extra time and horsemanship to bring out the qualities an average built horse has that come from their willingness to be a part of your plans. This is also where the statement "pretty is as pretty does" is born, by those people who have reached success with an ugly or not so beautifully shaped horse. Conformation is also where you will learn a whole lot about a horse's heart and will to participate, for some of the greatest horses ever known to equestrian sports and especially the notable ones in racing had major conformation flaws. This is also the department that you will learn how important owning a horse is that is correct in the legs will add to longevity in competition over a horse that has flaws which lead to extra stress points in the joints and tendons as you add more intense training and physical exertion. Understanding the basics of conformation will also help you to guesstimate what a horse will travel like and be capable of in their movements. This is a huge bonus if you are a trainer or would like to become a trainer, because some of the best horses are sold at auctions where there is no option to ride them first. You just have to know what you are looking at.

As an aspiring polo player or horseperson who wants to train polo ponies, it is essential that you understand the physical needs a polo pony will have and clearly understand that the foundation of any horse and especially the polo pony who is a tremendous athlete in all that they do, needs to have a solid foundation of legs underneath them and that starts at the hooves. Good conformation in the hooves and lower legs is crucial. That is the foundation that will carry you both, so pay attention to what the legs and hooves look like as a first priority on the list. You can a lot of times overlook extreme anomalies in body shapes if they have great leg conformation and are really correct. A correct horse, meaning in the legs front and back, will stay sound much longer than a beautiful bodied incorrect legged horse. That is an expensive lesson to learn and especially if you are the seller, as you need every single aspect of help when it comes to reaching the greatest sale price potential. When you start the process of training a polo pony and the product you have chosen as your prospect already has a few dings (or points of negotiation) due to a lack of a good leg foundation in its visible conformation, you are already seriously limiting your price potential no matter how slow you go in the training to ensure a good job. Buyers will always knock a horse on conformation when it comes time to negotiating and the veterinarian who will vet it will start right there as there first point of chatter. A veterinarian will start at the negative possibilities of what can happen long term based on their knowledge of injuries treatment due to conformation flaws. That is what a vet is there for, to help you know what to be on the lookout for. It doesn't mean that the injuries will "always" happen, but it does increase the likelihood when flaws are present.

I have owned some of the funniest built horses that turned out to be great polo horses and one in particular who was quite notable for his conformation that no other horse possessed was a 3-year-old brown thoroughbred gelding named Castle Buzz. But he had one unbelievable, well three unbelievable characteristics that made me pull the trigger and buy him. His body conformation looked like spare parts...literally, they didn't match at all. But, he had the absolute kindest and deepest eye and expression as I've ever seen in or on a horse...that was the prompt that hooked me first. The other conformation qualities he had were impeccably perfect legs and exactly as you would like to order them and a giant deep shoulder with a great angle for a smooth ride. He was a gem to train as he put his heart and soul into everything he was exposed to and was the smoothest and most honest horse to ride so I loved to ride him. He became a staple in my string and played everything I played in (8 goal, 10 goal, 14 goal, 16 goal, 20 goal, 22 goal, 26 goal) all the way up to the US Open and was a part of the 1999 CV Whitney 26 Goal winning team. He was the soundest and smoothest horse to play and always ready to put his heart and soul into the game. He then went on to be sold to one of America's top players and passionate horseman Dale Smicklas. D'Jeat was retired by Dale well into his teenage years sound and happy where he spent the rest of his life. I renamed him "D'Jeat", because of his funny looks and conformation when I bought him that caused everyone in the audience at the auction to erupt in laughter as he was led into the auction ring. D'Jeat stands for "did you eat yet" from Jeff Foxworthy's famous redneck jokes and that's exactly what he looked like when I bought him that night. He was purchased from a weigh pen at a by weekly auction after not making it as a racehorse. The first bid was from the slaughter buyer and the second bid was mine at $420 as the crowd laughed him out of the ring. My point, pay attention to conformation, but don't be surprised if that next diamond in the rough is not perfect in body shape.

The best point to make about the importance of conformation in a polo pony prospect is that what you are looking at visually will translate into certain physical qualities or inabilities that are the norm for a particular build of horse. Depending on what is your desired result is where conformation really matters. That is where you want to learn to match the right style conformation with the level horse you are trying to produce in your end results. Remember, great polo ponies come in all sizes and shapes, so it will benefit you to pay attention to the conformation of your current best horses and start evaluating the similarities they may have. Also remember that there are many different types of polo ponies that are needed for different levels of players, so that is a factor as well if you are looking to sell a horse to a particular level of polo which has specific demands.

One other point to keep in mind about conformation is this. I could get into a couple hundred more pages of actual conformation details that add up to good and bad qualities a horse is likely to have based on what it looks like in conformation, but the most important information you need to gather before saying if the conformation is good or bad is for what level of Polo is this prospect intended for? That is the first question to ask after the horse has been looked over in the eye (for sight issues) and leg department (correct and soundness). That is what will tell you if conformation matters or not. For example, if I am looking at a short necked mixed breed gelding about 14 hands high who has a great set of legs and a thick short neck and straight shoulder with not much girth to him…I am probably shooting myself in the foot if I think I am buying a high goal prospect who can run with the best of them and be sold at a high price. See what I mean. That gelding may be a top low goal horse or arena horse, because they are built for stability versus long-term speed and flexibility. This is an extreme example, but my point to make with you is you have to know what type of skills and Polo you want the horse for and then see if the traditional ideas attached to conformation notes match what you are looking to do. There are tons of books on conformation and why I did not choose to go into it here, so if you are new to conformation then give some time to researching it and then some time to the qualities "you" most like in the conformation points of a horse. That is what is most important, because just like a herd of pageant moms...everyone has an opinion on what is the best. What matters after soundness and leg structure is what is the type of horse you like to ride and the conformation qualities those horses possess? You are the one who will ride and perhaps eventually play it, so you have to like what you are working with and feel positive energy each time you work with them. That is how a trainer gets to the best results, not by owning what looks the part. The horse that looks the part in conformation is usually well suited for Polo, but it may not be your style depending on what you want to accomplish, so do some investigating until you learn the parts of conformation that are beneficial to your personal success and the desired results you would like to have with the finished product. If you are aiming your sales at the top of the sport than start looking through the barns of top players and the internet to see the similarities top ponies possess. Once you start looking you will start seeing common traits in conformation.

Importance of soundness in a new prospect

This part of the buying and consideration process is where you are creating the start point in injuries you will need to manage as you go or the ability to start free and clear of old injuries. Starting a horse for polo with no injuries will ensure your greatest chance at a high price when you go to sell them if you are a trainer. Starting with a sound prospect, free of injuries if you are making them for yourself will also ensure the greatest potential at a long career. Soundness will be a determining factor in you and the horse's overall safety during performance as well. You could have the greatest horse in the world, but because of soundness issues you are only able to get a few chukkers a season out of them before they need time off again. It is a process that is very expensive to repeat each season, because of the cost to maintain a horse monthly in stalls and the extra time in attention to details they will require as well in vet calls if you are unsure of your progress and need to know from an expert if you are getting it right.

The common question a whole lot of players have both amateur and professional is what to do when a new prospect they are considering has an old injury? Should you pass all together or give the horse a try? When you go to buy a new prospect the answer whether to buy it or pass depends on what your desired end result is. If your desired result is to eventually sell the horse at a high profit after training, you need to take a serious consideration to this one fact. Once a horse is a finished and seasoned horse when it is time to sell and the vet check comes…this old injury will be the first point of negotiation or cause to pass that comes up in the discussion between buyer and seller. It doesn't matter how much time or money you have in the horse, the buyer is looking for a horse with clean legs and this will be a huge hit to the price you had imagined getting. My point is this. If this is your business you may need to do some math before pulling the trigger on a previously injured horse as your new project if your intended result is a high profit. Figure 1-3 years of expenses for training, depending on what type of previous training this horse had and then add in your time and extra vet maintenance costs and see what you have in total potential expenses. Now match that to the price you think you could get for a "finished horse with this injury". That is how you will know of it is ok to buy a previously injured horse if this is your business. Tons of people learn this lesson the hard way and if you are depending on the horse for income you may come up short if you do not look at this one reality before you begin.

What I am pointing out are some really helpful guidelines to help you make the right decision for you and especially if you have high hopes to sell the prospect after training. Polo takes a certain amount of soundness for a horse to be able to do well and when you start with a horse who already has injuries, you are diminishing your chances at having a sound horse who can show up for every chukker during the season, unless you are a skilled professional or have a great groom who knows how to manage the daily care old injuries will need so that the horse can do its best.

Another big detail to know when considering the prospect that may have an old injury is what is the extent of damage? As we discussed earlier, is it cosmetic or part of the structural make up of a leg? That is a huge question to be able to answer and may need professional advice to know for sure. If you know what you are looking at in legs and injuries you may be able to read when a horse has a minor blemish that can be healed and not bother you one bit, but if you do not have this skill than you may want to seek professional advice when an issue arises in the soundness issues of a potential prospect purchase. Whatever you do, do not leave the question unanswered as it may bite you in the ass later if you proceed with no regard, because the horse is so pretty and cheap.

The bottom line is this. A prospect will need to be tested as they go through training for Polo. In order to really test a horse you have to be able to exert them to exhaustion physically and challenge their mentality through a series of training steps over time. Without being able to truly test a horse fully, because of always needing to be conscious of a previous injury or reoccurrences of flare ups, you may never be able to find out its full potential or be able to get to the finished product. These are just a few of the most important tips to keep in mind when considering purchasing a horse with previous injuries as a potential polo pony prospect.

8

Tips on Playing Unknown Horses

*Photo: by Sunny

Now we are going to have some real fun! Part of my career has involved the ability to get on completely unknown horses and be able to figure them out in less than 5 minutes and be able to perform even though I just met them 5 minutes ago. That is a skill that takes time to master, but one that every single polo player can benefit from, because at some point you will be trying horses to buy, or traveling to play with friends on their horses, or traveling to play where the horses are provided, or renting or borrowing a horse to get through a game and it makes a big difference if you can make the best of the situation. How much practice have I had at that? My whole life actually has been peppered with riding unknown horses and all over the world in my travels. One example in particular is when my career went in the direction of International matches and high profile events around the world, one season in particular I circled the globe on airplanes …literally, twice… and in that span I rode over 120 different horses combined. Some of the events I literally got off a plane into a driver's awaiting car and went straight to the field where we suited up and went to playing. What that means is you have about 5 minutes to assess the horse that is being led up to you by the groom who may or may not speak your language. The job then becomes how good at assessing the scene in front of you are you? Do you know how to read the finer details that are present in the type of bridle it has on, by the way they actually walk or jog to you, by the way the groom will or won't mention anything about them, by the way they are conditioned, by the way they are clipped or not clipped, by the way the martingale is adjusted and a million more details. I also gained a lot of experience riding the unknown horses through my years of buying prospects and doing one of my absolute favorite things to do which is to try to put the puzzle together of what a horse is all about by the way it is presented or not presented, to you the buyer. Once you are able to learn what to look for, it then becomes a skill to be able to see what the horse has to offer and what they do not want to offer when you get on their backs. If you can get to the right answer in a short amount of time, you can get to playing the game right away instead of riding the horse and wasting energy and time in a chukker trying to force what you are used to a horse doing to happen. Yes, you have to learn what is readily available and what is not an option at the moment. That is an art to master, but a completely necessary skill to attain to some degree of success as a player who wants to improve. To be able to get on a horse and be able to push its best buttons right away means you can have a great game, as opposed to not being able to read what is possible and spending the whole chukker fighting a giant Marlin you can't reel in. This skill matters to a player, so here are a few tips to always keep in mind that will help you with riding unknown horses. Enjoy, I learned them the hard way reeling in a school of wild Marlins and monsters in horse suits posing as polo ponies, but they are some of the most valuable lessons that paid off big time in reaching my career goals.

Bridles: Pay attention to what bridle the horse shows up in. The bridle usually indicates what the owner or head groom thinks of the horse and how difficult or easy they are to handle. Pay attention to **how they are adjusted** and where the martingale specifically is set. Is it tight to keep the horse's head down or adjusted in a place they can't get their nose out and away from so they can run off with you? Is it completely loose and a non-factor? It matters. Pay attention to if the bridle has a **mouth shutter** (drop noseband) or not and how tight the mouth shutter is or isn't. This is a good indicator of the issues an owner or groom may be having with the horse in a heated game where the horse is pressured. Generally speaking a horse that plays intentionally with no drop noseband is thought to have a light mouth and sensitive to the touch. Pay attention to if the horse is in **straight reins or draw reins** and if the draw reins are crossed over top of the shoulders which can indicate a control issue. Each type of rein is there for a reason and was put there to enhance control. Generally speaking a horse who goes in straight reins is more steady and easier to control than a horse who is put in draw reins. That does not mean horses who go in draw reins are all tough, it just means that the sign of straight reins on a horse generally means the owner or groom feels they are pretty straight forward and very simple to handle. Pay attention to the **length of a Pelham** shank and if there are any types of ports that are non-visible inside the mouth. Longer Pelham length usually indicates the horse has had stopping issues or is hard to stop. A high port inside the mouth usually indicates trouble stopping or a previously tough horse that is being brought back to a usable state with this extra hardware.

All of these small tips can help you know before you ever throw your leg over the back of the horse just what you may be in for, regardless of what you have been told. This is a huge heads up if you will take the time to pay attention to what is in front of you.

The horse's behavior: is the horse dragging its ass as they walk to you or are they literally dragging the groom with their nervous jig? Are they making circles back to where they were coming from or are they stamped with a lets get busy look of concentration as they pull up in front of you? Are they already sweating and the groom has not even warmed them up yet? There is a reason for sweat and it is usually from nerves or the horse has been literally ridden down so it will be quiet when it gets to you and the chukker ahead. Some horses may show up with some sweat because it is hot, but it will do you a big benefit to start learning how to spot the difference. Generally speaking a horse who is extremely nervous and shows up sweating will often times wear themselves out quickly in a chukker or have a need for you to treat them gently with less pressure when you are cuing for aids than other horses.

The groom or person bringing the horse: yes, this is always a fun and good indicator. Are they willing to answer questions? Are they proud of the horse or are they a bit nervous to engage with you in your questions? Yes, human nature over rules bullshit every time so trust your gut instinct. Don't be afraid to ask questions and watch the reactions. Are they willing to go warm the horse up for you so you can see what they go like? My favorite disaster in motion is when the groom will not look you in the eye or even answer what is the horse's name when I asked…true story and more than once. The tip there is get ready, because this could be a Halloween movie about to play out and the value of the ticket I just paid for by asking questions and paying attention to the answer is this… be prepared for anything. That's a tremendous piece of wisdom and it will help you in tricky situations to help unnecessary accidents from happening when you can prepare yourself properly with the right info before you begin. Here is a funny true story and what a great benefit transpired by asking questions about a horse before riding it and more specifically when a name rings concern or curiosity. I once asked the name of a cute little grey mare I was about to play and the answer was this. Her name is "Hellbitch". To which I immediately had lots of questions and thank God I asked them, because to this day that was one of the slipperiest, wild animals I have ever been on that has been sold as a finished "polo horse" into an unsuspecting beginner and sponsor's string. The reason the sponsor wanted me to play the horse was to assess if they were nuts or was this horse crazy as they suspected, but were being pressured by the seller that they just needed to learn to ride better it was a great horse. Hilarious chukker ensued as I attempted to play this horse in tournament polo, but the thank God moment came in the fact I at least had a warning by asking a few questions before I got on. My teammates were in hysterics watching me ride this what must have looked like a greased up dolphin who had a vicious deep-water dive and roll after the surfacing for air was done. Trust me when I say it pays to ask a few questions to the person who leads the horse to you and then pay attention to their response.

Your safety in the first unknown chukker: when you are getting on the unknown horse to play, make sure to give yourself about 1-2 minutes of the first chukker to try out the gears and see what the horse does and doesn't do before you go full throttle on what you want to do as a player. This way you can build a bit of confidence and discover the potential potholes before you are stretched out over the neck at full speed. This one tip can really help you assess a horse much better as well, because for the start of the chukker you will be focused on "what does this horse have to offer" instead of where's the ball and how fast can I get there? It is a much bigger confidence booster to the traveling polo player to utilize this strategy if you want to play your best game. Each time you can ride and get off of a chukker where you the player are able to get the most out of the horse instead of being intimidated by the entire chukker, you will be adding another layer of kick ass to your overall skill and that is extremely valuable in the hunt for improvement as a player.

Warm up: one of the best tools and tips to use when you travel or are trying horses is to ask the groom or handler to please warm them up for you. This way you will have a few minutes to assess a lot about the horse like: are they fresh or not, do they buck, do they have a mounting issue, what kind of stride they have when they canter, what their lead changes look like or if they are even able to make them, what their stop looks like, if they come off the ground when stopped hard or stay quite…it all matters. This is one of the absolute BEST tools to put in motion on your behalf, because a lot of the mystery is solved when you can "watch" the horse before you actually get on it. You will know right away if the horse has a huge stride and you prefer a short stride, you will know right away if they have a glitch turning one way or the other, you will know right away if they have a mounting issue, you will know right away if they actually stop nice or it's a nightmare to watch. So do yourself a favor and when possible, ask for the horse to be warmed up so you can assess the situation to your benefit before getting on. You may also want to give the horse a second to warm up when you do get on it and be sure and try out both directions of a turn and a full stop to see what kind of controls you will have and how much pressure it takes to get the correct response you are looking for. This is extremely valuable to know before you start the chukker.

Take a test drive when you first get on: the best way to find out quick what a horse wants to offer, what they naturally have and what they are not interested in offering is to trot them out to the field (so you can feel any unsoundness issues that will indicate potential turning difficulties one direction or the other depending on where the stiffness is) then hit a canter and let the horse go both directions in a circle and when ready a roll back in each direction. Don't try to help them too much, just see what is there at first and then you can add to it after you know the start point. This will let you know if the horse is left handed or right handed and how easy or hard it is to get an actual turn. Make sure that in your circles you hit one figure eight so that you can assess if the horse makes nice lead changes or not. You will also want to increase your speed just a little and go ahead and ask them to stop just so you know if they are going to pull on you or slam on the brakes champion Reiner style. This matters big time, because you as the player needs to know how much room you will need to make stops without fouling or getting in dangerous spots when you add speed. This small routine will help you assess a lot about a horse in one minute.

All of these tips are aimed at helping you discover the tell tale signs of what is to come in your upcoming unknown chukker. My overall point and advice you should leave this section with is this. Start paying attention to the small details and don't be afraid to start asking questions before you get on. There are many more to know, but these should get you started and are some really valuable ones that can add a lot of information to those unknown horses you will play before you even get on them. These tips will also help you to have a bit more confidence stepping into the next chukker with a completely new horse.

You should always keep this one piece of advice in mind when you are attempting to play any unknown horse, **your safety should come first**. That means if you will take the time to start learning about bridles and all of these small hidden clues and tools I am pointing out you will begin to set yourself up for a lot less mistakes, which can lead to buying a lot of beer or missing out on an entire season because you got hurt un-necessarily.

Another really big tip to give some thought to is this when it comes to playing the unknown horse. If you find yourself in a game where you are playing a horse that is seriously tough and you are expected to contribute as a player to the team, keep this tip in mind. Instead of trying to correct the horse and man handle them into doing things the way an easy horse would, which is where a lot of players will lose a tremendous amount of energy struggling, just focus on what the horse "can do" and use the talent it does have to offer, for that one chukker. You may have to adjust what you can normally get done and be a little more selective of which plays you enter into, but you will 100% exit the chukker with a whole lot more effective result in your help to the team and eventual outcome of the game if it is a tournament. This is the best way to get the most out of a tough horse and still contribute to the team. This will also help you conserve a whole lot of energy that can be lost due to nerves, failed expectations and frustration fighting this 1,000 monster in a horse suit. Knowing how to read the horses as you meet them and especially learning what they naturally have to offer as your first weapon to use when playing them takes time, but the skill will pay off immensely, especially if you are and aspiring professional or person who intends to travel and play tournament polo. It really pays off if you can grow this skill and especially if you can perform well under pressure on new horses. Take some time each new horse you ride to give these points I am making some attention and watch what begins to unfold right in front of you that you may have never noticed before. This is the way to building your own skill of reading unknown horses well.

9

Now let's talk about you…

Photo: Sunny's horses enjoying some turnout during the season to freshen up.

Now that I have explained a few of the absolute most important insider details that all top players know when it comes to their horses and doing their best as a polo player, it is time we talk about you and how you can start putting this information to use in advancing your own Polo. Getting to the top of the sport means you are going to dedicate yourself to learning all of the things you do not know, until you can master them with complete confidence. That process takes time and it takes focusing on the correct places to spend your time. Yes, you have to first know what is the right information to pay attention to and where is your time best spent. That is if you want to get somewhere before you are too old to do anything about it. That is why the time you will spend learning the horse element and your relationship with them is the key to everything. That is the point of this first book on the topic. Horses are everything to your own success as a polo player no matter what your personal goal is. That is why it is going to be so important to start breaking down the key ingredients that make up the relationship you need to have with your horses into very digestible chunks of food that you can eat as you go and are ready for. Think of it like an enormous buffet…you will be eating for a while so pace yourself and focus on what most intrigues you first. That relationship is everything and actually the word relationship that I am trying to describe to you is meant to mean everything that goes along with the horse aspect of your game. I mean everything and there is a reason I mean everything, from your time spent in riding singles, to the time you spend learning the best fitness plan for your horses, to the time you will spend with your grooms to assess what is happening with a particular horse, to the time you spend at the tack shop trying to find the exact right bridle to improve that challenging horse or size of reins to help you control them better, to the time you will spend with the vet trying to figure out the best maintenance strategy for an injury so you can have your best mare at the important games, to the time you will spend on the practice field, to the time you will spend at the mallet shop trying to get the right length mallets for your horses, to the time you will spend stick n balling and finding out who does well with stick n ball and who doesn't need it or like it, to the time you will spend in tournament chukkers learning the depth of what your horses have to give and the time you will spend in frustration trying to figure out why your horses aren't keeping up with your opponents as you race down the field…all of it. All of it equals what I am attempting to describe in the word "relationship" and is the space where you can gain a tremendous amount of ground as a player. With each new piece of knowledge you gain, you will be adding one more layer of confidence to you the aspiring polo player. That is how greatness is built…one solid brick at a time.

Now that you know some key points of what to start paying attention to you can start applying what appeals to you currently or has hit a cord of sharp interest and see where it takes you. I guarantee it will land you at one step ahead of where you were and that is the path to progress. Each step forward counts, so get to work and enjoy the process of discovery as you go. It can be quite rewarding when you hit a huge breakthrough with a certain horse or a new level of confidence you find like after you are able to clearly determine the value of knowing your style of horse and what it will add to your game potential.

Always remember what I am pointing out in the benefits of paying attention to the small details that can improve your confidence on the field. Most of them boil down to what is coming from your horses and your ability to interact with them on the field. Yes, that one component underneath it all…the confidence they bring you or take away from you. If you take away one major point from this first book on the topic of polo ponies, make it this one.

"Your horses are the foundation for your abilities on the field, because of the level of confidence they can provide that equals your willingness to take chances and give it your all."

Without that, you will always be severely limited in your potential as a player. There is no other source of input you can seek as a player that adds up to the power that comes from there.

All of these details I have explained will effect people in different areas, so just give some consideration to what I am saying and start looking around you at the top players in your club and their horses as well as what goes on at their barns. You will be able to see for yourself if what I am saying exists in these concepts I have explained, that are at the root of all top players success. I am quite confident that once you know what you are looking for, you will start to see the similarities I am talking about and that is something to truly learn from and why I felt the need to explain these often very hidden details in this first book on polo ponies. If you are seeking to hit and compete in the top of the sport as was my goal, there is no time to waste when it comes to getting your horses right. You have to be an absolute detail freak and that means especially when it comes to the horses. They are everything to your success.

Always remember this advice if your progress begins to slack off at some point. Getting things right between the type of horses you are playing, what you need to be able to get out of them in a game and what you can do to help your team in the game means everything. If you can't contribute to the overall performance of the team in a positive way, you need to start looking at why you can't? Is it a certain chukker that you can't help or is it your whole game? Start there and then start collecting clues until you get to the answer that can help you go forward, now that you know what you are looking for.

My goal in this first book on polo ponies is 100% aimed at helping you, the player, see the effect the horses you are playing are having on you that you may have never considered before or known about. I hope after reading this you realize how much value lies in the horses you are playing if you know how to look at it properly with the right information that is proven to work. Having the right information means you can repeat the results in a success.

Good luck with your own string and make sure to give your horses all the extra time you have so you can develop the best relationship possible and the one that brings you the most enjoyment in the sport.

That's all…now get to the barn and start assessing the scene for clues to your potential growth. ☺

10

Who is Sunny Hale?

Photo: Sunny Hale in action by Chris Yeo / Kuala Lumpur

Sunny Hale is the first woman in history to win the US Open Polo Championships, the author of 5 books, a professional speaker and a 2012 National Cowgirl Hall of Fame inductee alongside American icons who have helped shape the American West such as Sandra Day O'Connor, Georgia O'Keefe and Patsy Cline.

The New York Times called Sunny
"the most famous female polo player in the world".

ESPNW compares her accomplishment as
"Some say she's pulled off the equivalent of being the first woman to earn a World Series Ring."

Sunny is widely recognized among her peers both male and female, as the most accomplished and well respected female Polo player in the world. What sets her apart from the pack, is her achievements at the top of what has traditionally been a male dominated sport and the fact that she was hired to compete on polo teams for over 20 seasons alongside some of the greatest male players of all time, as a professional among them. Her most famous victory in Polo is the day she became the first woman in history to win the US Open Polo Championships, American Polo's most coveted trophy and title as a professional player. For that historic win that has ignited a movement in polo around the world for women, she was hired by the Outback Steakhouse Polo Team at the request of the world's #1 player of all time Adolfo Cambiaso. This would be the equivalent of a woman being hired to play in the NBA, World Series or the Super Bowl as a starter among the men and winning the championships. With no template to follow, she not only achieved her personal dream, in what has been called the second most dangerous sport only to auto racing, but she amassed one of the most impressive winning records and literally changed history forever in the process.

In 2015 she created an educational platform for aspiring polo players called Let's Talk Polo. The educational platform includes expert advice, insider details, tips and wisdom she learned along the way in her professional career that is suitable for polo players of all skill levels. As of 2016, the platform includes a 3 book series (Let's Talk Polo, Let's Talk About Your Handicap, Let's Talk Polo Ponies) as well as social media access on Instagram and Facebook where players can find professional wisdom and tips from a legend in the sport.

Sunny is currently working on the book about achieving her dream in the sport of Polo, called "Conquering the Dream". Interest in the new book and her story of achieving success in a male dominated profession, has already taken Sunny around the nation and internationally in professional speaking opportunities.

Wins and Special Awards in Professional Polo
(partial list)

US Open 26 goal: Outback Steakhouse Polo Team
Adolfo Cambiaso, Sunny Hale, Lolo Castagnola, Phil Heatly
*Tim Gannon- team patron

CV Whitney Cup 26 goal: Lechuza Caracas Polo Team
Pite Merlos, Sebastian Merlos, Victor Vargas, and Sunny Hale

Hall of Fame Cup 22 goal: Outback Steakhouse
Adolfo Cambiaso, Gonzalito Pieres, Sunny Hale, Tim Gannon

Ylvisaker Cup 22 goal & MVP: La Dolfina / Newbridge
Adolfo Cambiaso, Sunny Hale, Matias Magrini, Russ McCall

Sterling Cup 22 goal: Calumet Polo Team
Eduardo Heguy, Nachi Heguy, Henry DK, Sunny Hale

Robert Skene 20 goal: Goshen Polo Team
* voted by players **MVP Robert Skene Award**
Owen Rinehart, Julio Arellano, Sunny Hale, Ervin Abel

Bondell Cup 20 goal: Audi Polo Team
Gonzalito Pieres, Sunny Hale, Melissa Ganzi, Juan Bollini

Texas Open 20 goal & MVP: Bob Moore Cadillac
International Cup 16 goal: Sympatico Polo Team
Palm Beach Polo & Country Club 14 goal League

Win of special note:

Don King Days…the famous Buckle, Sheridan Wyoming!

Wins and Special Awards Women's Polo
(partial list)

7 Time Polo Magazine Woman Player of the Year

US Women's Open 1990, 2011, 2013 & MVP

WCT Finals 2006, 2007, 2009, 2010, 2011, 2012 & MVP

First Royal Malaysian Ladies Championships 2012

USA vs. Argentina at Palermo Field #1

ICWI International Ladies Tournament Jamaica

Argentine Women's Open 1999

Thai Polo Queen's Cup 2012

Dubai International Ladies Tournament
*under the patronage of Sheikha Maitha al Maktoum

National Sporting Library Supermatch 2014 ,2015 &MVP

Argentine Women's Open 2015
*La Dolfina: SH, Mia Cambiaso, Cande F Araujo, Milagros F Araujo
Coaches: Adolfo Cambiaso & Milo F Araujo*

Founded by Sunny Hale

Let's Talk Polo
Educational platform for aspiring polo players
Facebook.com / LetsTalkPolo (polo tips)
Instagram.com / LetsTalkPolo (polo tips)
Amazon.com/author/sunnyhale (books)
Kindle (e-books)

WCT (Women's Championship Tournament)
International women's polo league founded in 2005
Mission: new friendships, good polo…shared passion.
www.wctwomenspolo.com
Facebook.com/WCTwomenspolo

American Polo Horse
Created in 2006 to recognize polo ponies in America.
Facebook.com/AmericanPoloHorse

To learn more about author Sunny Hale go to:
www.sunnyhalepolo.com

Additional books by Sunny Hale

Available at amazon.com/author/sunnyhale

Let's Talk Polo

Let's Talk About Your Handicap

How to Gain Confidence as a Rider

I want to be a Champion

Copyright Sunny Hale 2016

All rights reserved. No part of this work may be reproduced in any form without the written consent of its author.

www.sunnyhalepolo.com

www.ingramcontent.com/pod-product-compliance
Lightning Source LLC
Chambersburg PA
CBHW030112010526
44116CB00005B/215